Kitchens

Anne McKevitt worked in the fashion industry, first as a hair stylist, then as a stylist for magazines such as *Vogue* and *Elle,* before a career change to run her own successful interior design company. Her first book, *Style on a Shoestring*, was full of good ideas for creating stylish, fun rooms without spending a fortune. Anne makes regular appearances on BBC1 and BBC2 and is the regular designer on *Home Front.* She lives in London.

home front

Kitchens

Anne McKevitt

BBC Books

To Don for constant love and support
My mum, video expert – not

Principal photography: Mark Nicholson, Shona Wood
and Paul Bricknell
Other photography: Colin Poole and George Taylor

This book is published to accompany the
BBC Television series *Home Front*.

Series Producer: Mary Sackville-West
Editor: Daisy Goodwin

Published by BBC Books, an imprint of BBC Worldwide Ltd.,
Woodlands, 80 Wood Lane, London W12 0TT.

First published 1998

ISBN 0 563 38391 7

Edited and designed for BBC Books
by Phoebus Editions Ltd

Art Direction: Anne McKevitt
Styling: Anne McKevitt
Assistant: Kay Hawkins

Set in Futura
Printed and bound in France by Imprimerie Pollina s.a.
Colour separations by Imprimerie Pollina s.a.
Cover printed by Imprimerie Pollina s.a.

Contents

Foreword 6
Introduction 7

THE MAKEOVERS 10

The Small Kitchen 12

Planning 14
The look 16
Instant countertop 17
Striped units 18
Mosaic splashback 20
Storage and display 22
Painted cork flooring 24

The Family Kitchen 26

Planning 28
The look 30
Painted pine units 32
Handles 35
Recycled worktop and splashback 36
Traditional sink and taps 38
Details 39
Dining area 40
Vinyl floor tiles 42

The Cook's Kitchen 44

Planning 46
Cooking area 48
Tiled splashback 51
Woodgrain units 52
Deep worktop 54
Sink area 55
Key details 56
Colourwashed floor 58
The larder 59
Utility room 60

The Glass Kitchen 62

Planning 64
The look 66
The units 68
Paintwork 70
Woodstrip flooring 72
Mobile storage 73
Textures 74

THE ESSENTIALS 76

Units 78
Storage 80
Worktops 82
Splashbacks 84
Sinks and taps 86
Appliances 88
Lighting 90
Flooring 92

Acknowledgements 94
Index 96

Foreword

In the TV series *The Waltons* the kitchen is the heart of the home. For some, this is true but for an awful lot of us it is a fantasy. Don't forget that the kitchen is just another room whose importance varies from person to person. You may find this hard to believe, but I've had several clients who insisted on not having kitchens under any circumstances in their houses. I persuaded them, if only for the purpose of resale.

What's fundamentally important is what kind of kitchen suits you and your needs. It's not there to impress the mother-in-law or the neighbours, no matter how tempting that is. Cooking and eating are enjoyable pleasures for many of us, while for others food is simply fuel that is a chore to prepare.

My first appearance on *Home Front* was doing a makeover on three kitchens. Since then I've tackled every room in the home and survived, but I'm still passionate about kitchens.

Introduction

A kitchen is a living room and must reflect your lifestyle, not someone else's. There's no point in a busy young couple having a family kitchen, or someone who loves to cook having a minimalist preparation place. It's just common sense.

You can spend a fortune on a new kitchen, so unless you've just won the lottery, the first thing you have to do is decide how much you are willing to spend. Don't forget to include the cost of installation in your budget, which is usually as much as the price of the kitchen itself.

Before you design your kitchen, you need to think about how you cook, where you eat and whether anyone helps you with the cooking. If you like cooking and baking, then you will need a lot of storage, plenty of worktop for concocting masterpieces and a larger than normal oven and hob. If you have a young family and the kids eat their meals in the kitchen, you've got to plan for that.

When you've decided on your budget and the function of your kitchen, it's time to work out the design. The best way I know of getting inspired is to rummage through books, magazines and newspapers, tearing out pictures of anything that you could possibly want in your kitchen.

ABOVE: THE EFFECT OF THE HIGH-TECH STAINLESS STEEL AND CHROME ACCESSORIES IS EMPHASIZED BY THE NATURAL TEXTURE OF THE EXPOSED BRICKWORK.

Don't limit yourself just to articles on kitchens: inspiration can come from the most unlikely of quarters and the more inspiration you have, the better. Then you can start to focus on what you like, and begin planning.

The word planning may sound a little on the professional side, but don't be put off or scared. All it means is gathering your thoughts, looking for inspiration, measuring up and taking on board plumbing and electrics which are the mechanics and workings of a kitchen.

Before deciding on the capacity of units that you require, you will have to assess your needs. Do you want your appliances to be integrated or on view? Will the oven be in the traditional position in a base unit or will it be at eye level? Do you need a large fridge-freezer or will a small one suffice? Do you need a large sink if you've got a dishwasher?

Before you go to your local superstore or kitchen outlet, do some careful forward planning. Spend lots of time accurately measuring the room. Do all your measurements in metric as this is what most kitchens are sold in. Draw a rough sketch of your room with the measurements marked on it. Then draw rough elevations showing everything from the height of the ceiling to the width, height and location of doors, windows, radiators, plumbing outlets and electrical sockets. Ask your plumber and electrician to come round simultaneously to discuss

ABOVE: EVERYTHING COMES BACK INTO FASHION EVENTUALLY. HERE, THE RETRO FIFTIES LOOK FINDS A MODERN SETTING, WITH ALL THE CONVENIENCE OF TODAY'S FITTINGS AND APPLIANCES.

ABOVE RIGHT: THE NEW KITCHEN CHARACTERISTIC IS FLEXIBILITY. THIS MOBILE UNIT CATERS FOR AN EVER-CHANGING KITCHEN DESIGN.

ABOVE: THE CLASSIC UNFITTED KITCHEN, HAND-MADE AND LOOKING LIKE A PIECE OF FURNITURE. IT HAS AN INGENIOUS RANGE OF HEIGHTS AND SURFACES FOR EVERY POSSIBLE USE.

your plans. They will be able to tell you whether what you have in mind is possible, and, if not, offer alternatives.

Take all this information with you when you head to your local super-store. They will do drawings on a computer for you of the kitchen you want. These drawings are incredibly helpful in visualizing your kitchen, and you can anticipate any difficulties before you have it installed. Beware of keen-talking sales people who work on a commission basis, and don't commit yourself there and then. Take the drawings home and make sure that the design is what you really want.

Books, magazines and kitchen shops keep going on about the work triangle rule, which I think is a myth – your kitchen should reflect how you work. For example, if you drink a lot of cold drinks, you'll want the fridge close to the door and glasses nearby. If you have pets, the cupboard where their food is kept is one that you'll be in and out of more often than others. Remember, it's your kitchen and as such should cater to your needs and reflect your style.

RIGHT: A LARGE SPACE DOESN'T NECESSARILY NEED TO BE FILLED. A MINIMAL NUMBER OF UNITS AND APPLIANCES GIVES AN AIR OF COOL URBAN CHIC.

THE SMALL KITCHEN 12

THE FAMILY KITCHEN 26

THE COOK'S KITCHEN 44

THE GLASS KITCHEN 62

The Makeovers

Dull, cluttered and tatty may sum up your kitchen at home. But once you've read this book, which shows four very distinct makeover projects, achieved on varied budgets, you'll see that anything is possible. You can decide then whether to rip out your tired old kitchen and start afresh, or maybe just spruce up your exisiting one with daring and imagination.

In designing this kitchen there were two restrictions – lack of space and a tight budget. However, the big bonus was that the units could be treated like a blank canvas.

The *Small* Kitchen

In this kitchen I wanted to prove that you can have stylish design that is trendy and of the moment, using non-standard colours, without it looking absurd or tacky. It also shows that small can be beautiful.

The painted stripes, mosaic splashback and colourful accessories give the kitchen its fun, quirky personality, but their visual impact depends on efficient storage. In such a small space the secret is to get all the clutter out of the way first.

I designed the kitchen for a recently married couple. They were on a tight budget but, in fact, that actually worked to their advantage, since inexpensive, very basic units were just what were needed. The units had no features of their own to detract from the colourful stripes.

ABOVE LEFT AND RIGHT: BASIC WHITE BUDGET UNITS WERE PAINTED IN A RIOT OF COLOUR, WITH A MULTI-COLOURED MOSAIC SPLASHBACK LINKING THE LILAC AND MAUVE STRIPES.

Planning

Never think of a small kitchen as a poor substitute for one the size of a football field. With planning and ingenuity, you can have a kitchen that is much easier to work in than a large one – and a lot cheaper to furnish.

A galley layout is the ideal arrangement here, as it allows most things to be within arm's reach of each other, along with a good run of worktop on both sides. There is ample storage, too, as the layout was planned to provide maximum capacity in minimum space. The units are far enough apart to allow them to be opened comfortably from both sides at once – essential in a galley layout.

BELOW: THE INSPIRATION FOR A FUN, LIGHTHEARTED KITCHEN DOESN'T ALWAYS COME FROM THE OBVIOUS.

14

To go with the horizontal stripes, I wanted a graphic style for the splashback and flooring that would not look too fussy. Simple patterns were important, because too much detail can be difficult to live with. I settled on random mosaic tiles for the splashback, combined with cork tiles painted in a pattern of alternating triangles for the flooring.

Although one of the owners is a professional caterer, fancy gadgetry wasn't required, as she didn't want the kitchen to resemble her workplace. A free-standing cooker and dishwasher were chosen so that the couple can take these with them if they move home in a few years' time.

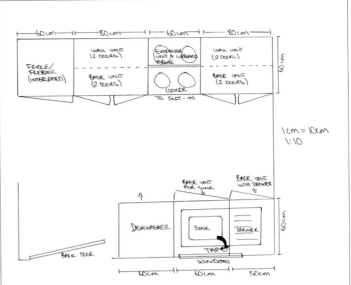

ABOVE: WHEN PLANNING A KITCHEN, DO A VERY BASIC FLOORPLAN TO WORK OUT YOUR LAYOUT. THE LEAST COMPLICATED WAY IS TO USE A SCALE OF 1 CM TO 10 CM (OR 1/2 IN TO 5 IN).

LEFT: THE KITCHEN AT THE HALFWAY STAGE, WITH THE UNITS INSTALLED. ALL THAT'S NEEDED NOW IS A SPLASH OF PAINT.

15

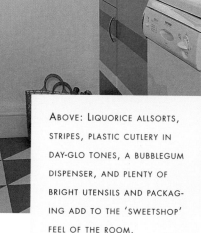

ABOVE: LIQUORICE ALLSORTS,
STRIPES, PLASTIC CUTLERY IN
DAY-GLO TONES, A BUBBLEGUM
DISPENSER, AND PLENTY OF
BRIGHT UTENSILS AND PACKAG-
ING ADD TO THE 'SWEETSHOP'
FEEL OF THE ROOM.

The Look

After talking for hours to the young couple who own this kitchen I decided it couldn't be run-of-the-mill. They wanted a unique look, within the constraints of budget and space. The galley layout lent itself well to horizontal stripes, in candy colours inspired by Liquorice Allsorts, painted on to the units. This design set the atmosphere for the room, developing into a sweetshop/soda fountain look with lots of kitsch accessories, like Day-Glo plastic cutlery.

To get the right look I considered all the elements – cabinets, flooring, worktops, splashback, wall and details. All these mixed together with a dash of wit and humour created this inventive, sleek and efficient kitchen.

Instant Countertop

One of the challenges in this kitchen was how to create enough worktop space in a small area, so I designed an additional, fold-down countertop. Not only does it provide an extra metre (three feet) in a well-lit area, but it also makes a perfect spot for a quick snack. A hinged section of worktop, it can be quickly lowered into place across the door when needed.

The windows in the door and behind the sink shouted out to be dressed simply but ingeniously. These clever blinds, with holes cut in the fabric, give an extra textural feature to something that would otherwise be bland. They are more sensible than curtains.

ABOVE: ACCESS TO THE BACK DOOR IS UNOB-STRUCTED WHEN THE FOLD-DOWN WORKTOP IS LOCKED IN AN UPRIGHT POSITION.

LEFT: THE FOLD-DOWN WORKTOP IS IDEAL AS A BREAKFAST BAR. BECAUSE THERE ARE NO UNITS UNDERNEATH IT, THERE IS PLENTY OF LEG ROOM. THERE'S A GREAT VIEW INTO THE GARDEN, TOO.

Striped units

The kitchen doors on the units used here are laminate, so the surfaces have to be given a 'key' prior to painting to help the paint adhere. This is generally done by lightly rubbing them down with sandpaper. I used oil-based eggshell paint, which is ideal for kitchen woodwork as it is very hard-wearing and has a slight sheen.

Painting the units with horizontal stripes emphasized the galley layout and at the same time made it look bigger because there are no solid blocks of colour defining a specific area. There is one floor-to-ceiling unit, housing a large fridge-freezer. The stripes help it to blend into the surrounding units, stopping it looking too bulky for such a small room.

To decide the width of the stripes, I drew them first roughly on the fridge-freezer unit because it is the tallest and also because it is in a corner. I then marked them exactly, starting at the bottom and working my way up. The stripes have to be absolutely straight and even, so I used a ruler for measuring and marking out and a spirit level to ensure the stripes were level. I then masked along the lines so they would be straight. (Low-tack masking tape is best because it's less likely than ordinary masking tape to pull off the paint when removed.) I then worked my way round the kitchen, regularly checking with a spirit level.

It is easier to prime and paint the doors if you unclip them first and lay them flat, but they need to be hanging in position while the stripes are marked out.

ABOVE: PAINTED STRIPES IN UNCONVENTIONAL COLOURS DISGUISE THE BASIC NATURE OF THESE BUDGET UNITS. BECAUSE THE LAMINATE SURFACE IS NOT POROUS, 'KEYING' THE SURFACE IS ADVISABLE.

YOU WILL NEED...

Patience! • *Fine-grade sand-paper* • *Primer and white undercoat* • *Small roller and small decorator's brush* • *Ruler, spirit level and pencil* • *Low-tack masking tape* • *Eggshell paints in two tones*

1 *Rub down doors; wipe clean. Using a roller and brush, paint on primer; when dry, apply undercoat. Starting at bottom and using ruler and pencil, mark widths of stripes on doors. Lightly pencil in the lines using a spirit level.*

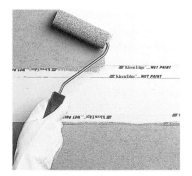

2 *Mask lighter stripes, continuing tape around sides of doors. Paint the sides using a brush, then paint fronts with a small roller.*

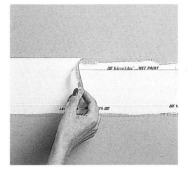

3 *When dry, apply a second coat of same colour if required. While that coat is still damp, carefully peel off the tape.*

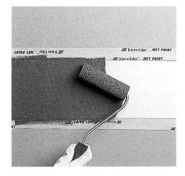

4 *Mask the edges of the darker stripes and paint these in same way.*

Mosaic splashback

Although mosaic tiling looks like a job for a professional, it is incredibly easy, particularly when there is no pattern, only a random mix. The tiles do not have to be fixed individually, as they are already stuck to large paper squares which protect the fronts of the tiles and are peeled off after fixing them. Because the splashback area is small, using mosaic here was stylish but relatively inexpensive.

> ### YOU WILL NEED...
> *Knife or scissors • 30 cm (12 in) square sheets of mosaic tiles in assorted plain colours • PVA glue and cotton bud • Tile adhesive and spreader • Sponge and cloth*

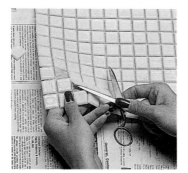

1 *Using a knife or scissors blade, remove some chips from each mosaic sheet, without tearing the paper.*

2 *Using PVA glue and a cotton bud, glue a random selection of tiles face down on to each sheet.*

3 *Use spreader to apply an even, 3 mm- (1/8 in-) thick layer of tile adhesive to portion of wall where mosaic is to be applied.*

ABOVE RIGHT: ALREADY-MIXED RANDOM SHEETS OF MOSAIC ARE AVAILABLE ONLY FROM A SELECT FEW TILE SHOPS, BUT IT'S VERY EASY TO DO ON YOUR OWN.

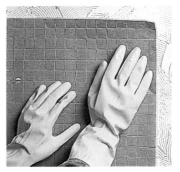

4 With paper on top, press first mosaic sheet into the adhesive. Position other sheets in same way, being careful to align rows and columns of tiles on adjacent sheets. Leave to dry for 24 hours.

5 Dampen paper using a wet cloth or sponge then peel it away from tiles.

6 Sponge on the grout over the tiles, pressing it well into the gaps between them. Wipe off excess grout with a damp cloth.

Storage and display

As we all know, kitchens seem to generate enough paraphernalia to do a manned mission to Mars. The owners of this kitchen have to be very disciplined about what gets put where, since storage space and display areas are at a premium. Only constantly used items and appliances deserve prime

positions and anything that has to be stored on the walls or the worktop has to be a pleasure to look at. The professional-type shelving by the window is decorative as well as functional. It is used to store large items like trays, colanders and storage jars, while utensils are hung beneath the lower shelf, which saves on drawer space. Too often you feel there is a magpie in the kitchen, hiding all the household junk in the drawers, but here the owners decided they would need only one drawer, which is used for cutlery. This in turn meant more space for cupboards. A small integrated extractor, rather than one with a hood, was fitted over the hob, again to save space.

Accessories are to a kitchen what jewellery is to a black dress. I made the four display boxes on the wall to emphasize the look and colours of the kitchen.

ABOVE: THE ONLY ACTUAL STORAGE UNIT ON THE WINDOW SIDE OF THE KITCHEN CAN BE CLEARLY SEEN IN THIS 'BEFORE' PICTURE, NEXT TO THE GAP FOR THE DISHWASHER.

RIGHT: METAL SHELVING PROVIDES EXTRA STORAGE SPACE, WITHOUT MAKING THE KITCHEN SEEM TO BE BURSTING AT THE SEAMS AS A WALL UNIT MIGHT.

YOU WILL NEED...
*Wooden display boxes •
Sandpaper • Matt emulsion
paint, decorator's brush and
cloth • Glue gun • Items to
fill boxes – I used plastic cutlery and straws, liquorice
strips and dried seaweed*

HOW TO MAKE
DISPLAY BOXES

1 *Lightly sand boxes. Mix
one part paint to five
parts water. Brush on to boxes
and lightly wipe off excess
with damp cloth. Leave to dry.*

ABOVE: THE LOOK OF
UTENSILS ON DISPLAY IS AS
IMPORTANT AS THEIR
FUNCTION.

LEFT: FILL DISPLAY BOXES
WITH ITEMS THAT ARE APPRO-
PRIATE TO YOUR DECORATIVE
THEME AND USE THEM AS
ACCESSORIES ON ANY SPARE
WALL SPACE.

2 *Use glue gun to stick
items in place. Leave
boxes flat so that items will
stay in position as glue dries.*

Painted cork flooring

In this kitchen the limited budget meant that I had to come up with a stylish yet inexpensive solution to covering the floor. I chose cork tiling, which might seem surprising, since to many people cork says just three things: dull, dull, dull. Yet cork tiles are inexpensive, hard-wearing, resilient and warm underfoot – and I could paint them to create a simple yet dramatic design.

The pattern of alternating triangles of grape and white complements the graphic use of stripes on the units and the rectangles of the mosaic splashback.

The cork tiles are painted before they are laid and varnished afterwards. After preparing the sub-floor (see page 42), spread cork tile adhesive using a spreader to ensure that you get an even level of adhesive across the floor. Only spread about one square metre (square yard) at a time. Too much or an uneven amount of adhesive on the floor will result in adhesive oozing out of the joins and ruining the surface of the tiles. Press each tile into position, butting the edges and smoothing out any trapped air.

Normally, cork tiles are laid starting from the centre of the room and working outwards. Here, however, I started along the line of the units by the cooker because I wanted the grape to look as if it was coming out from under the plinth. I then worked my way across the room.

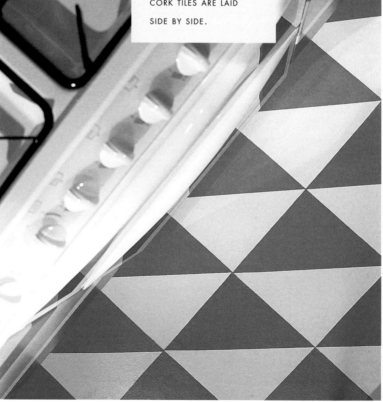

BELOW: THE SIMPLE TRIANGULAR SHAPES PAINTED IN WHITE AND GRAPE LOOK REALLY DRAMATIC WHEN THE CORK TILES ARE LAID SIDE BY SIDE.

YOU WILL NEED...
Unsealed cork tiles • Low-tack masking tape • Emulsion paint in white and grape • Small decorator's brush and paint tray • Artist's brush for touching up marks • Acrylic varnish and brush

1 Tiles are painted before being laid. Stick masking tape diagonally across each tile, running your finger along tape edge to ensure it is well stuck down.

2 Paint half of the tile white, brushing away from tape to prevent paint from seeping underneath. If necessary, apply second coat after first has dried.

3 Carefully remove tape while paint is still damp; if dry, it could come off with tape. Allow to dry completely.

4 Stick tape over diagonal edge of white half, leaving 1 mm of white showing beyond tape.

5 Paint grape half of each tile as in step 2. Remove masking tape and allow to dry thoroughly.

6 When laying tiles, be careful not to dirty the tops. Touch up any marks with paint. When dry, apply several coats of acrylic varnish, allowing it to dry between coats.

TIP

Where possible I use acrylic varnish, because it is water-based and dries quickly, so you can apply several coats in a day. It is also water-proof, non-yellowing and environmentally friendly.

This modern country-style kitchen avoids the twee natural-pine look often associated with country style. Though comfortable, welcoming and natural, it is also upbeat.

The *Family* Kitchen

To most people, except those who actually live in the country, the image of a country kitchen is natural wood, most likely pine, from top to bottom. Pine doors, pine table, pine chairs and pine dresser – basically very boring and lacking imagination.

The owners of this kitchen are a family who come from rural Ireland and now live in the city. They loved the country look, but decided, after some persuasion, to go for a modern version of it.

Even though the kitchen is large, it was kitchen hell and the space was badly utilized. Storage space was inadequate, and worktop space non-existent. In fact, the only working area was on top of the washing machine. Alongside the freestanding cooker was a base unit, but there was a microwave oven on top of it, with a kettle and toaster on top of that.

ABOVE LEFT AND RIGHT: THE ORIGINAL KITCHEN WAS DESPERATE FOR A REVAMP. IT IS NOW CHIC, COLOURFUL, INTRESTING, TEXTURAL AND YET STILL INTRINSICALLY A COUNTRY KITCHEN.

Planning

When so much renovation is needed, the prospect can be quite daunting, particularly as there are often severe physical (not to mention budgetary) restrictions. This kitchen, believe it or not, was literally designed around a table which was cumbersome and bulky and didn't collapse. The owners were desperate to keep their pine table, even though it was completely out of proportion. I hated it – one, because it was pine, and secondly because it was so large.

In addition, I had to design around a room that was long and narrow and that had no less than three doors leading into it, none of which could be closed off or

LEFT: THE ORIGINAL KITCHEN WAS DOMINATED BY DOORS THAT WERE USED FREQUENTLY.

BELOW: THE PLAN SHOWS HOW THE PENINSULA THAT HOUSES THE SINK AND DISHWASHER, AND HALF THE TABLE, DIVIDES THE KITCHEN INTO TWO SEPARATE AREAS.

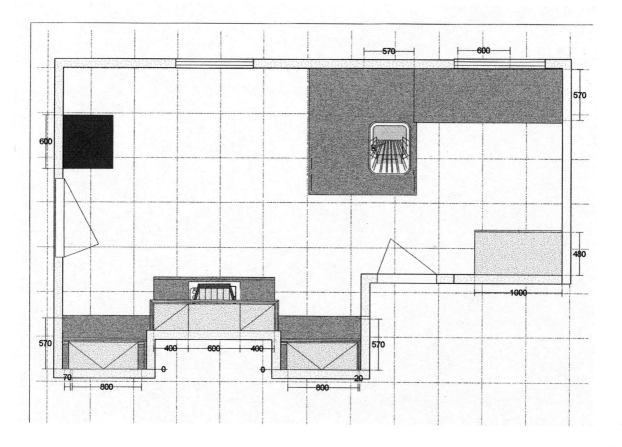

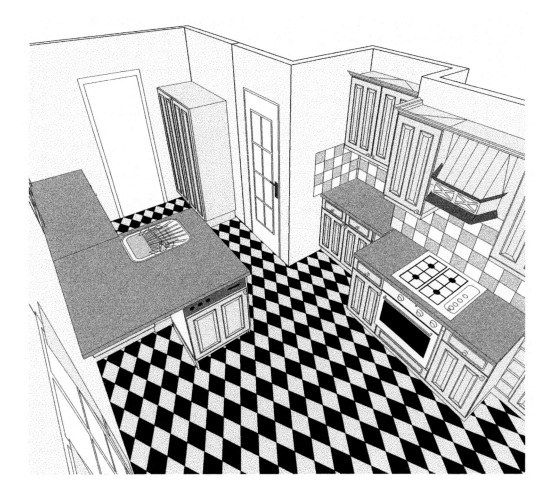

moved. I had not only to leave access through all three, but also to allow for freedom of movement between them. To cope with all three problems, I decided to incorporate an unusual peninsula unit in the design. The end consists of a housing for the dishwasher, but between that and the wall is an area the table can be slid into. With half the table hidden, it is much more in scale with the kitchen. There is enough room for two people to eat at the table, and it is easily pulled out when seating is required for up to six people. A sink is also sited in the peninsula unit, backing on to the dishwasher. The washing machine is on the adjacent wall, so that the plumbing only

ABOVE: THE SPACE UNDER THE WORKTOP OF THE PENINSULA INTO WHICH HALF THE TABLE CAN BE SLID IS CLEARLY VISIBLE HERE.

has to run to and from the one place. The peninsula divides the room into two sections, with the sink, dishwasher and washing machine in one area, and the cooking, preparation and eating in the other. Each area is of a manageable size, yet the traffic flow between the three doors is not obstructed.

To do this I had to move the kitchen from one side and end of the room to the other, which meant moving the services. However, it has made such a difference to the room that it was well worth it.

BELOW LEFT: LIKE A
PHOTOGRAPH FROM THE
LAST CENTURY – HOW THE
KITCHEN LOOKED BEFORE
RENOVATION.

BELOW: TRADITIONAL ITEMS
LIKE THE BELFAST SINK
EMPHASIZE THE
TIMELESSNESS OF THIS
MODERN COUNTRY KITCHEN.

The Look

The country kitchen can all too often look stale and uninteresting. To give it a new, fresh, bare-faced optimism I decided on a French provincial meets New England look. What a country kitchen shouldn't be is twee. Nothing looks worse than dusty dried flowers hung from mock timber-clad ceilings. I grew up in the wilds of Scotland and, believe me, this image doesn't represent country life.

Rustic wood, the hallmark of many country kitchens, looks warm and homely but you can have too much of a good thing. Pine is often over-used, so much so that you can't see the wood for the trees. The family who live here loved bare wood, and their original kitchen had a pineclad ceiling, pine doors, windows and skirtings, and a pine table and chairs. I wanted to prove that we could get rid of all of that and yet still have a country-style kitchen – one that would be fashionable without dating quickly, and would be chic yet at the same time comfortable, earthy and textural.

I also wanted to show that all this can actually be achieved with shop-bought rather than custom-made units. Often, all that is needed is to spice them up with

some colour. The family liked the door shape and the style of these pine units, so we used them on the strict understanding that they would be painted and colour-washed in two rich shades of red and yellow ochre.

giving surfaces a different texture than they would normally have. Here, old slate roof tiles were cut and used for the splashback, and 150-year-old floor-boards were recycled as the worktop. Because it is the only natural wood in the kitchen, this old pine is more noticeable and its beauty fully appreciated.

The traditional country kitchen would originally have had a large black range, so I decided on a black oven and hob which have a slightly old-fashioned appearance. The details such as the oven door handle and knobs are brass, which echo the brass sink taps.

Accessories like the old scales add an authentic touch, and the black-and-white vinyl floor tiles complete the look without the chilly feel of original marble tiles.

BELOW: THE OLD AND THE NEW PLAY WITH COLOUR, SHADOW AND TEXTURE.

The easy option is to buy everything brand-new but often you can miss out on the authenticity that comes with age. This is the time to look at the least obvious choices for the special details. Using unusual materials can be very effective,

Painted pine units

The wonderful thing about the size of this kitchen is that it allowed me to go for an abundance of units for storage. None of the units are fitted with carousels or pull-out larder units – because of the space available, it was

more cost-effective to purchase extra basic units with simple internal shelving. The units I chose are from a superstore and are made from solid wood rather than less expensive laminate. The two bottle racks on either side of the oven area were an extravagance within the constraints of the budget. The sloped front of the extractor with the forged iron grille breaks the uniformity of the units and helps to identify the cooking area. The expanse of worktop is now enormous. (Remember that originally the only preparation space was on top of the washing machine!)

When you are out shopping for a kitchen, don't be put off by the colour of a particular door if you like the style of it. The colour can be changed. I customized the standard solid-pine doors that came with the kitchen by using two strong but warm shades of red and yellow ochre. It was like painting a large blank canvas, and it would have been overwhelming in just one colour – the contrast between the two shades makes it much more interesting.

I created further interest by painting the outer parts of the doors with a wash and the recessed panels with undiluted paint. You can still see the grain of the wood around the outside, which enhances the texture of the cupboards.

ABOVE LEFT: ORIGINALLY, THE PINE TABLE DOMINATED ONE END OF THE KITCHEN, LEAVING LITTLE ROOM FOR FITTED UNITS OR ANY OTHER FORM OF STORAGE, WHILE THE ALCOVES ON EITHER SIDE OF THE TABLE WERE COMPLETELY WASTED.

RIGHT: SIMPLY MOVING THE TABLE MADE ENOUGH SPACE FOR A WHOLE WALL OF STORAGE AND WORKTOP, WITH THE HOB AND OVEN IN THE MIDDLE OF IT. SETTING THE UNITS INTO THE ALCOVES MADE IT ALL LOOK MORE VARIED AND INTERESTING.

HOW TO CUSTOMIZE PINE UNITS

1 *Unclip each door from its hinges and lay it flat on newspaper. Rub down doors with sandpaper, and wipe them clean. This helps to create a key so paint will adhere well.*

2 *Mix one part of matt emulsion paint to three parts water. Apply this colourwash with brush to outside part of one door, brushing in direction of grain. (There is no need to mask off recessed panel at this stage.)*

3 *After a minute or two, wipe over colourwashed area with dry kitchen towel to remove some of the wash. Repeat the colourwashing for the other doors.*

4 *When wash is dry, mask around edges of recessed panel. Now apply primer to this panel, using the brush. Repeat for other doors.*

5 *When primer is dry, paint each panel with solid, undiluted colour. Carefully peel off masking tape from doors while paint is still damp.*

6 *When paint is completely dry, apply a coat of acrylic varnish with a different brush. If you expect heavy wear, apply two more coats of varnish, allowing it to dry between coats.*

Handles

The style of handles on the units can make or break a kitchen. Simply changing the handles can greatly alter the whole style of the room. There is an enormous variety to choose from, so take care to select some that suit the look you are after. If your units have been supplied with handles that are not quite right, don't hesitate to replace them with others that look better.

In this kitchen chrome handles would have been completely out of place, while brass ones would have been too precious and prissy. The black forged-iron handles I chose are perfect. With their rough edges they look like something a blacksmith might

ABOVE: I CHOSE CHUNKY, UNFUSSY FORGED IRON HANDLES TO COMPLEMENT THE COLOUR-WASHED WOOD AND THE SLATE SPLASHBACK OF THIS KITCHEN.

have made. They are very much in keeping with the natural country theme of the kitchen.

LEFT: HANDLES FOR KITCHEN CUPBOARDS AND DRAWERS ARE AVAILABLE IN AN INCREDIBLE RANGE OF SIZES, STYLES, SHAPES, MATERIALS, FINISHES AND COLOURS, INCLUDING FORGED IRON, BRASS, COPPER, BRUSHED STEEL, CHROME, GLASS, RESIN, PLASTIC, CHINA AND WOOD.

Recycled worktop and splashback

Because it's the only area of bare wood in the kitchen, the worktop stands out very much as a feature. Using 150-year-old pine floorboards – found in a salvage yard – has given it a marvellously textured and lived-in finish. The tops were sanded enough to get rid of the dirt and to ensure they were hygienic, but not so much as to remove the characterful indentations that a century and a half of use brings.

To make them level, the undersides of the floorboards were planed – planing the top would have removed all the character. Because they are only half the depth of a

ABOVE RIGHT: THE NATURAL COLOURS AND TEXTURES OF THE WORKTOP MADE FROM RECYCLED PINE FLOORBOARDS AND THE SPLASHBACK MADE FROM RECYCLED SLATE ROOF TILES COMPLEMENT THE COLOURWASHED UNITS. THEY CREATE A PUNCHY COUNTRY LOOK THAT IS NOT THE LEAST BIT TWEE.

YOU WILL NEED...
Old floorboards • Coarse and fine-grade sandpaper • Wirewool • Beeswax

HOW TO FINISH A WOOD WORKTOP

1 Sand worktop, first with coarse sandpaper and then with a finer grade. Remove sawdust. Apply beeswax.

2 When the beeswax is dry, buff worktop to a slight sheen with wirewool.

normal worktop, the boards were fixed to large sheets of plywood. Next, the plywood-backed boards were then cut to size just like a normal worktop. The exposed edges were then covered with thin strips of wood cut from the floorboards.

For a waterproof but still natural-looking finish with a slight sheen, the surface was treated with wax. Every six months or so it has to be resanded and rewaxed. The waxing is quite hard work, but it's worth it in the end – the more you rub, the better the outcome.

I based the design of the slate splashback on a traditional American picket fence. Made from reclaimed slate roof tiles, the splashback took a professional tiler a day to make. It was well worth the expense since the textures and colours of the wood and slate offset each other perfectly. And, of course, it is also extremely hard-wearing.

The tiles were cut using an angle grinder. Grey grout was used between the slates rather than normal white. To prevent splash marks and stains, the surface was treated with a sealant which is available from any tile shop; this also gives the slates a slight sheen.

ABOVE RIGHT: THE MAYHEM THAT WAS THE ORIGINAL KITCHEN, WHEN THE ONLY WORK SPACE WAS ON TOP OF THE WASHING MACHINE AND THE SPLASHBACK CONSISTED OF UNEXCITING WHITE TILES.

RIGHT: THE NEW KITCHEN SEEN FROM THE SAME ANGLE AS ABOVE, BUT NOW WITH ACRES OF WORKTOP AND A DRAMATIC SPLASHBACK.

Traditional Sink and Taps

The Belfast sink and twin-stem brass taps are a classic combination. The porcelain-coated fireclay of the sink is both heat- and stain-resistant, though crockery breakages are higher unless you use a plastic bowl inside it. Being deeper than normal, the sink is ideal for washing large pots and pans and baking trays. The antique-style mixer tap looks in keeping with it and gives good water coverage to all areas of the sink.

ABOVE: A BELFAST SINK, WITH ITS FRONT EXPOSED TO VIEW, IS TRADITIONALLY PART OF THE COUNTRY LOOK. ITS WHITE ENAMELLED FIRECLAY LOOKS WONDERFUL AGAINST THE RECLAIMED PINE WORKTOP.

LEFT: IT IS IMPERATIVE TO SEAL THE JOIN BETWEEN THE BELFAST SINK AND WORK SURFACE USING A CLEAR SILICONE SEALER. OTHERWISE, THE SIDES OF THE WORKTOP WILL STAIN AND EVENTUALLY ROT.

BELOW LEFT: A DRIED-LEAF
PICTURE IS INEXPENSIVE TO
MAKE AND IS UNIQUE.

BELOW: A HANGING POT-
RACK ADDS ANOTHER
DIMENSION BY UTILIZING THE
CEILING FOR EXTRA STORAGE.

Details

What you hang on the walls, or even from the ceiling, adds atmosphere to the room. In this

kitchen I hung saucepans from a pot rack and made up some framed pictures for the walls using a selection of dried leaves in colours that echo those of the units.

YOU WILL NEED... *Piece of hardboard*
• Red emulsion paint, water and kitchen cloth
• Dried leaves, flowers, seedheads, fruits or spices, plus nuts, twigs, curled balsa-wood or other natural materials • Glue gun
• Wooden frame

HOW TO MAKE A LEAF PICTURE

1 Dilute one part paint with about three parts water and apply to hardboard using kitchen cloth.

2 Arrange main pieces of dried material on hardboard in a pattern you like and secure in place with glue gun. Allow some leaves to extend beyond edges.

3 Fill in gaps with decorative bits of wood, glue-gunning in position in same way. Secure in frame, with leaves at edge overlapping frame.

Dining area

The large pine table was stained a peacock blue and repositioned next to one window, making dining a more pleasurable experience. The shutters make the difference between okay windows and fabulous ones. They are the only ornate items in the kitchen, and are wooden fretwork. The sides were spray-painted white and then masked off while the detailed inserts were sprayed light grey.

ABOVE: THE WINDOWS ORIGINALLY HAD CURTAINS – A BIG NO-NO IN A KITCHEN BECAUSE THEY ARE LIKE MAGNETS FOR GREASE, DIRT AND STEAM AND CAN BE A FIRE HAZARD.

RIGHT: THE SHUTTERS AT THE WINDOWS GIVE PRIVACY YET LET IN THE DAYLIGHT, CASTING BRILLIANT SHADOWS ACROSS THE KITCHEN WHEN THE SUN IS SHINING. THEY MAKE AN ATMOSPHERIC BACKGROUND TO THE BLUE TABLE.

ABOVE: THE LARGE, NATURAL PINE
TABLE HAD TO BE ACCOMMODATED IN
THE NEW KITCHEN.

RIGHT: STAINING THE TABLE BLUE AND
REPLACING THE WOODEN CHAIRS
WITH BRIGHT BLUE MODERN ONES
RUBBER-STAMPED THE CONTEMPORARY
LOOK OF THE KITCHEN.

YOU WILL NEED...
*Coarse and fine-grade
sandpaper • Colourglaze
(coloured wood stain and
varnish mixture) and brush*

HOW TO STAIN A WOODEN TABLE

1 *Sand table, following
grain. If table is very worn,
use coarse paper first,
finishing with fine-grade.*

2 *Brush on colourglaze, with
grain. Allow to dry, then
lightly sand and apply another
coat. Repeat with one or two
more coats, depending upon
depth of colour required.*

Vinyl floor tiles

YOU WILL NEED...
Metre ruler and pencil • Vacuum cleaner • Self-adhesive vinyl tiles • Chalk and scissors

Practically any unit, table or chair that you place on top of these traditional black-and-white floor tiles will look impressive. They are one of the all-time classical flooring designs for kitchens, and they contrast with the colourwashed red and yellow ochre base-unit doors and the bright blue table.

Self-adhesive vinyl tiles are practical and also easy to install, and can be laid on either a wood or a concrete sub-floor, so long as it is smooth and level. (If not, cover uneven or gappy floorboards with hardboard fixed with hardboard pins. Cover rough concrete with a screed of self-smoothing compound.) Seal concrete with a sealant such as diluted PVA.

HOW TO LAY VINYL TILES

1 Prepare sub-floor. Mark out centre of floor using metre ruler and pencil. Vacuum floor to ensure there is no dust or grit that will damage tiles when they are walked on.

2 Plan your layout, starting from centre of floor. Remove paper backing from a few tiles.

3 Position tiles, sticking them firmly to floor and ensuring that there are no gaps between them. Continue until entire floor is covered, cutting them as necessary (see Tip).

TIP

If you need to cut any tiles, mark cutting lines on them with chalk, and cut with scissors before removing the backing. Leave the backing in place until you're ready to stick the tiles down.

BELOW: THE BLACK-AND-WHITE
TILES LOOK DRAMATIC AGAINST
THE RICH RED, YELLOW OCHRE
AND BLUE USED IN THE KITCHEN.

Everyone loves to eat and most of us love to cook. This kitchen was created for a passionate cook – someone who loves cooking and whose every spare moment is spent in her kitchen preparing food.

The *Cook's* Kitchen

The primary aim in redesigning this kitchen was to ensure that the layout as a whole and each individual unit would function efficiently. Accessible storage and uncluttered work surfaces were key factors, with the look being secondary in importance.

The principal difference between this kitchen and the others in the book is that all the main elements are exaggerated and made larger to cope with the bustle of cooking. There is an extra-wide oven, a five-ring hob, unusually deep work surfaces and more storage space than most of us could fill in a lifetime.

The utility room off the kitchen was rarely used, and so I designed it to double as an area where snacks and hot drinks could be prepared by any member of the family without interrupting the cooking.

ABOVE LEFT AND RIGHT: THE CLUTTERED HELL OF A BADLY DESIGNED KITCHEN WITH TOO LITTLE WORK SPACE WAS TRANSFORMED INTO THE PERFECT KITCHEN FIT FOR A SERIOUS COOK.

Planning

There is no set recipe for a perfect cook's kitchen. Like any delicious meal, improvisation is the key to success. This despairing cook had a kitchen that needed a radical change. Chaos, disarray and confusion were the order of the day. Prior to the refit the only worktop and food preparation area was between the hob and window. This was also where the kettle and toaster were located, which meant that whipping up meals was continually being interrupted by other members of the family making tea and coffee and getting snacks. There was a breakfast bar opposite the oven but it was a wasteland and was never used. There was next to no storage in the kitchen.

The original oven was located at eye level just inside the kitchen door leading from the hallway. This was a hazard when the oven was being loaded or unloaded. The utility room resembled a garage rather than an annexe to a kitchen, and the floor was lower than that of the kitchen. The owner also had a very large collection of ceramic and plastic pigs everywhere, which added to the mayhem on the worktop.

The new kitchen was designed to afford the maximum work space possible for the owner. None of the services (water and gas) or the boiler was moved. The breakfast bar was consigned to a skip, and tall pull-out storage units and a fridge-freezer were planned in its place. It was decided to get rid of the original tall unit that housed the oven and have base and wall units in its place. Next to that a

large-capacity cooker was installed. An
extra-deep worktop was fitted to
maximize the work area. A mobile unit
with a granite top was constructed and
placed in front of the boiler. The old vinyl
flooring was binned, the concrete floors
were levelled and more appropriate
parquet flooring was laid.

RIGHT: UGLY POWER POINTS DOMINATED THE
BROWN TILED SPLASHBACK OF THE OLD KITCHEN,
SO I MOVED THEM WHERE THEY WOULDN'T BE SO
NOTICEABLE, UNDERNEATH THE WALL UNITS.

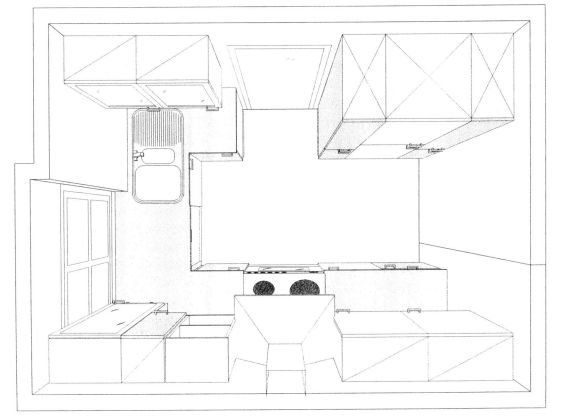

OPPOSITE AND ABOVE: COMPUTER DRAWINGS LIKE
THE ONES PREPARED FOR THIS KITCHEN HELP YOU
VISUALIZE EVERY DETAIL, SO THAT YOU CAN
ACHIEVE THE MOST EFFICIENT DESIGN. IMAGINE
OPENING THE DOORS OF THE UNITS, TO SEE IF
THERE WILL STILL BE ACCESS.

Cooking Area

Cooking doesn't just involve the activity that takes place on the hob or in the oven – ask any cook. In any kitchen dedicated to cooking the cooker itself is the axis around which all activity rotates, and so requires as large as possible a preparation area on either side, with ingredients and utensils all close at hand. Preparation can take an inordinate amount of time, and it's frustrating if you haven't got enough room.

I therefore included here a generous worktop on either side of the cooker, which provides space for resting dishes as they go into or come out of the oven.

ABOVE: THE WIDTH OF THE COOKER ALLOWS FOR A VERY LARGE, MULTI-FUNCTION OVEN AND A FIVE-BURNER HOB.

LEFT: FREQUENTLY USED INGREDIENTS ARE ALL WITHIN EASY REACH OF THE HOB, WITHOUT TAKING UP MUCH ROOM. THE RECIPE BOOK HOLDER IS NOT ONLY OUT OF THE WAY BUT ALSO AT THE RIGHT HEIGHT FOR READING.

RIGHT: HOOKS ARE USED TO HANG THE PANS AND UTENSILS FROM THE CUSTOM-MADE RACK MOUNTED ON THE WALL ABOVE THE SPLASHBACK, CLOSE TO THE HOB YET OUT OF THE WAY OF COOKING SPLASHES. THE RACK ALSO FREES UP A BASE UNIT FOR OTHER PRIORITY STORAGE.

BELOW: EACH SIDE OF THE COOKER IS USEFUL PREPARATION SPACE. UTENSILS THAT CAN'T BE HUNG UP, LIKE WOODEN SPOONS AND KNIVES, HAVE THEIR OWN NEAT HOMES HERE.

Spices are kept off the worktop in a wall-mounted spice rack. Bottles and jars of sauces and condiments frequently used in cooking are kept on a small lazy susan, and with one spin can be located at a glance. Salt and pepper are in two large pots to the side of the hob. There's even a special holder for recipe books at a convenient height for reading. A large, custom-made saucepan rack mounted high on the wall keeps pans within easy reach and in full view all the time for quick selection. It also frees up a unit for other storage needs.

The cooker itself is a freestanding 90 cm- (36 in-) wide stainless-steel model. Its five-burner gas hob and large-capacity electric oven with built-in grill and rotisserie can cope easily with any demands placed on it, from family meals to large-scale entertaining.

The cooker has been fitted with a safety rail around the hob to stop pans from being knocked over. A safety rail is essential for any family with children but it is a sensible precaution for everyone and will hopefully become a standard feature of hobs.

To deal with cooking smells, steam and grease, an efficient extractor is a must, and in a hard-working kitchen like this, it is even more of a necessity. The powerful vented overhead extractor hood I chose is literally conducive to a pleasant atmosphere. Extractor hoods work best if they are on an outside wall, but if they aren't, they can be ducted.

ABOVE: THE ULTRA-RAPID CENTRE BURNER OF THE HOB IS FOR WOK-COOKING, WHILE THE SMALL BURNERS ARE FOR SIMMERING. THE SAFETY RAIL STOPS PANS FROM BEING KNOCKED OVER.

The splashback behind the hob is stainless steel, which is easier to clean and more hygienic than a tiled splashback and therefore more suitable for this area. Some cooker or extractor suppliers offer ready-cut splashbacks, or it can be cut to size by a metal fabricator or a company that specializes in stainless steel products. All you need to do is bring them a cardboard template of the shape you want (see page 75).

Tiled splashback

Glazed tiles make an attractive and practical splashback behind the worktop or sink. I used hand-made tiles, which are thicker and more irregular than machine-made ones. What makes them unique is that each is marginally different from the others. When choosing tiles, bring samples of paint colours so that you make the right choice.

YOU WILL NEED...
Plaster filler, sandpaper, primer-sealer or emulsion • Tile adhesive and notched spreader • Glazed tiles •Spacers (see Tip) • Tile-cutting tools (see step 4) • Grouting (see Tip) • Plastic squeegee, sponge and cloth • Silicone sealant

1 *Remove any wallpaper or flaking paint. Fill cracks, sanding it smooth. Seal new plaster with primer-sealer or emulsion, or sand or score a painted wall. Ensure surface is smooth, clean and dry.*

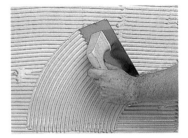

2 *Use spreader to apply an even, 3 mm- (1/8 in-) thick layer of adhesive where the first six tiles in bottom row will go; start at centre and work outwards, so any partial tiles will be at edges.*

3 *Press first tile in place, with bottom resting on worktop. Add other tiles in row and subsequent rows in same way, placing spacers between corners of tiles and making sure all surfaces are flush.*

4 *To cut tiles, score along cutting line on glazed surface using jig or tile scorer; place matchsticks under line, and press to snap in two. (For thick tiles, use heavy-duty cutter.) To cut intricate shape or curve, use pincers to nibble it away.*

5 *Leave to dry for 24 hours; remove spacers. Use squeegee to spread grout. Clean surface with damp sponge as you go. Polish off powdery residue with dry cloth. Seal join between tiles and worktop with silicone sealant.*

▼ TIP

Hand-made tiles must be spaced farther apart, as they are quite uneven. Instead of ordinary spacers, make your own by breaking up cheap machine-made tiles into 1.2 cm (1/2 in) squares (see step 4).

For grouting hand-made tiles, you will need to use special wide-joint (or flooring) grout.

Woodgrain Units

The outdated fitted kitchen was replaced with laminate units in two colours, natural and forest green, both with a noticeable wood grain. Not only have many more units been fitted into the same space, but the wall cupboards go almost to the ceiling, providing useful storage in what would otherwise be a dead area.

Another dead area was the space in front of the boiler, so, after moving the radiator, we hid the boiler with a mobile unit. For this we adapted a standard base unit by fitting

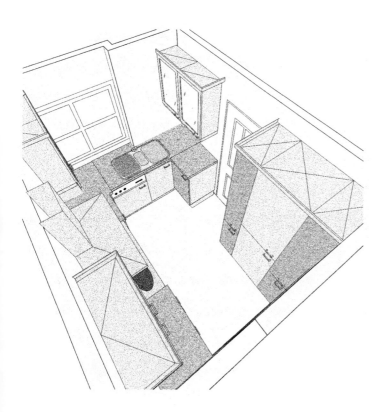

ABOVE: AS THIS COMPUTER DRAWING SHOWS, THE NEW UNITS MAKE FULL USE OF EVERY BIT OF SPACE, INCLUDING THE AREA IN FRONT OF THE BOILER, WHICH WOULD HAVE BEEN PROHIBITIVELY EXPENSIVE TO MOVE.

BELOW: THE SHELVES OF THE PULL-OUT UNITS ON EITHER SIDE OF THE INTEGRATED FRIDGE-FREEZER HAVE RAILS SO THAT NOTHING FALLS OFF.

ABOVE: THE GRANITE WORKTOP OF THE MOBILE
UNIT IS IDEAL FOR PREPARING PASTRY, WHILE THE
BAKING IMPLEMENTS ARE STORED INSIDE.

LEFT: THE CASTORS
ON THE MOBILE UNIT
HAVE RUBBER WHEELS
TO PROTECT THE
FLOOR, AND BRAKES
TO HOLD THE UNIT
IN PLACE.

industrial castors on the bottom, which
allow it to be easily moved in order to
gain access to the boiler. A high-quality
granite worktop was fixed to the top –
because granite is always cool, it is ideal
for pastry-making.

The fridge-freezer is invisible inside its
housing, and on either side of it are two
full-height pull-out larders.

Deep Worktop

The work surface around the sink is 80 cm (32 in) instead of 60 cm (24 in) – 20 cm (8 in) deeper than usual. This is breakfast-bar depth. The extra depth creates lots of extra space for preparing fruit and vegetables while still leaving room for an indoor herb garden in a pot. The window has intentionally been left undressed to allow maximum daylight in and give an unimpeded view of the very private garden.

LEFT: THE EXTRA-DEEP LAMINATE WORK SURFACE NEXT TO THE WINDOW ALLOWS THIS CORNER TO BE THE FOCAL POINT OF THE KITCHEN, BOTH FUNCTIONALLY AND VISUALLY. THE WINDOW, WHICH IS NOT OVERLOOKED, HAS BEEN INTENTIONALLY LEFT BARE TO ALLOW IN THE MAXIMUM AMOUNT OF DAYLIGHT AND TO MAKE THE MOST OF THE VIEW OF THE GARDEN. THE WINDOW FRAME WAS PAINTED IN THE SAME COLOUR AS THE DEEP-GREEN UNITS.

Sink Area

A dishwasher is essential in this busy kitchen as otherwise dishes would pile up in and around the sink, stopping it and the worktop being used for food preparation. Where you place your dishwasher is important: it needs to be near the sink so that it can be loaded easily after the dishes are rinsed, without dripping water all over the floor. It's also cost-effective to make use of the existing sink plumbing. In addition, you need a space to stand when you are emptying the dishwasher and a work surface to put clean dishes on.

BELOW: THE FLEXIBLE HOSE WITH SPRAY ATTACHMENT SIMPLY RETRACTS INTO THE MIXER TAP WHEN NOT IN USE.

ABOVE: MOVING THE SINK TO THE RIGHT AND THE DISHWASHER TO THE LEFT CREATED A BIGGER WORK SPACE IN THE AREA BETWEEN THE SINK AND THE HOB, MAKING IT SO MUCH EASIER TO LOAD AND UNLOAD THE DISHWASHER.

This sink is made from enamel. I chose a versatile yet compact design with one-and-a-half bowls plus a drainer. Fruit and vegetables can be washed in the separate 'half-bowl', using the clever retractable spray hose on the mixer tap.

The niche behind the sink drainer is the ideal space for a utensils rack complete with kitchen-roll holder.

Key Details

Plan your kitchen right down to the last detail. No matter how well planned the layouts or expensive the units, it is the details that will determine whether a kitchen is successful or not.

Because this is an activity room, lighting is of paramount importance, and all the more so in a kitchen designed for a keen cook who needs to focus on the job in hand. This kitchen was originally lit by a single fluorescent strip, which gave it

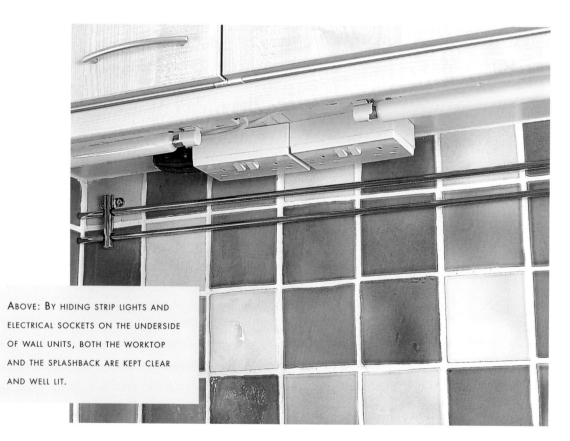

ABOVE: BY HIDING STRIP LIGHTS AND ELECTRICAL SOCKETS ON THE UNDERSIDE OF WALL UNITS, BOTH THE WORKTOP AND THE SPLASHBACK ARE KEPT CLEAR AND WELL LIT.

LEFT: HALOGEN TRACK LIGHTS CAN BE INDIVIDUALLY DIRECTED EXACTLY WHERE THE LIGHT IS NEEDED, YET THEY USE EXISTING WIRING.

BELOW: PUT THE BIN WHERE YOU NEED IT MOST — BESIDE THE COOKER — BUT HIDDEN IN A BASE UNIT. WITH ONE SWEEP OF YOUR HAND, ALL THE WASTE FROM FOOD PREPARATION IS OFF THE WORKTOP AND INTO THE PULL-OUT BIN.

the atmosphere of a dingy industrial canteen. I replaced the unfriendly fluorescent strip with halogen track lights, which give off a clean, bright, sparkling light that is closer to natural daylight than any other form of lighting. By directing one of the lights onto the oven and hob you get reflected light from the stainless steel extractor and splashback which increases the overall light level.

The hob is illuminated by a light built into the extractor hood and the worktops are lit by small tungsten strip lights fixed to the underside of the wall units, where they are hidden by the plinth. The necessary but unsightly electrical sockets are also located out of sight here. This keep all the appliance cables off the worktop and out of the way, and also avoids vandalizing the beautiful tiles.

The bin can easily be hidden too. We added a bottom to a normal unit, bought a fitting so the whole cupboard can be pulled out and adapted the door, which originally would have been hinged. This allows the bin to be sited next to the hob and preparation area where it is needed – which means no more traipsing across the floor, hands full of vegetable peelings, dropping bits everywhere.

Colourwashed floor

The parquet floor came from a sustainable forest. After colourwashing the floor, I painted a cartoon pig on it because the owner was besotted by them!

> YOU WILL NEED... *Parquet flooring • Cork expansion strips • Parquet flooring adhesive and spreader • Mallet or hammer and wood offcut • Tenon saw • Emulsion paint, water, decorator's brush and soft rag • Eggshell acrylic varnish and brush*

ABOVE: THE GREAT THING ABOUT WOOD IS THAT YOU CAN COLOUR-WASH IT ANY SHADE YOU LIKE WITHOUT COVERING UP THE GRAIN.

1 *Prepare sub-floor (see page 42). Starting at longest wall, apply adhesive and leave for 30 minutes. Lay first block, leaving 12mm (^{1}/2in) gap at the skirting. Press down, then tap all over with mallet or hammer on wood offcut. Repeat with other blocks, ensuring that edges butt up tightly.*

2 *To cut blocks for edges, use a tenon saw. Fill in gaps at skirting boards with cork expansion strips. Mix up colourwash in proportions of one part emulsion to five parts water.*

3 *Paint colourwash over an area a metre (yard) square, using loose, irregular brush strokes in all directions. The wood grain should still show through.*

4 *After a minute or two, wipe off most of the paint with a damp rag. Colourwash rest of floor in same way, avoiding hard edges. Allow to dry completely. Brush on several coats of varnish, allowing each to dry before applying next. (Acrylic varnish dries quickly, so you can do several coats in a day.)*

The Larder

Like most people, you probably have a cupboard that is full of what can politely be called junk. You don't need it and you'll never use it again, so get rid of it! The understairs cupboard adjacent to this kitchen was once filled with ski boots and other rarely used items. The junk was removed and, with minimal expense, shelves were fitted, transforming what was once a complete waste of space into efficient and spacious storage. This in turn freed up space in the kitchen for utensils and ingredients that are used on a regular basis. The shelves are shallow, which means that items don't disappear to the back out of sight. Always remember that one of the most important things when it comes to planning storage is visibility.

Non-perishable foods, drinks and cooking ingredients of all sizes and shapes, preserving pans, outsize salad bowls and other bulky pieces of kitchen equipment, as well as wine bottles in racks and a collection of cookery books, can all be fitted into a cupboard like this, so long as you think carefully about the spacing of the shelves. Try to keep any large, heavy items on the floor or lower shelves, since taking down heavy weights from a high shelf can be difficult. Less frequently used items can go higher up.

INSET AND ABOVE: WHAT WAS ONCE A WASTE OF SPACE HAS BECOME A WALK-IN LARDER NEXT TO THE KITCHEN, PROVIDING A VALUABLE STORAGE AREA FOR FOOD AND INGREDIENTS, DRINKS AND COOKERY BOOKS.

Utility Room

The utility room next to the kitchen had become simply an overspill area, housing not only the washing machine and tumble dryer but also odds and ends from the kitchen. By organizing the storage in the kitchen and utility room better, I was able to turn this under-used room into an annexe of the kitchen with a dual purpose. Though primarily a conventional laundry room, it also became a useful refuelling area for the family. Tea, coffee, an electric kettle and an assortment of snacks are now stored here, leaving the kitchen itself free for serious cooking.

ABOVE: THE FINISHED UTILITY ROOM, NOW A PROPER KITCHEN ANNEXE. WITH ITS FLOOR-TO-CEILING UNITS AND TILED SPLASHBACK, IT'S A FAR CRY FROM HOW IT WAS BEFORE.

LEFT: THE DISORGANIZED CHAOS OF THE UTILITY ROOM BEFORE THE REFIT — A PLACE FOR NOTHING AND NOTHING IN ITS PLACE.

ABOVE: THIS RECYCLING BIN HAS
SEPARATE COMPARTMENTS FOR EACH TYPE
OF INORGANIC WASTE.

BELOW: A RECYCLING BIN FITTED TO A
CUPBOARD DOOR IS CONVENIENT FOR
ORGANIC WASTE, TO USE FOR COMPOST.

To provide visual continuity, the utility
room cupboards were replaced with units
and a worktop matching those in the
kitchen, and the same tiles were used for
the splashback. A housing for the laundry
appliances allows them to be stacked one
on top of the other. Alongside, a tall unit
provides a home for an ironing board
and iron, along with mops, dustpans and

brushes and other equipment and
cleaning materials. A laundry basket is
stored in a separate mobile unit fitted
with lockable castors. A hinged lid lifts up
to give easy access to the laundry inside.

Also inside some base units are
recycling bins for paper, tins and cans,
glass, and plastic. Recycling bins should
be considered in every kitchen design.

A new conservatory and kitchen were the striking ingredients used to give a new dynamism to this traditionally decorated house and the lifestyle of its owners.

The *Glass* Kitchen

The starting point here was my radical suggestion of a new conservatory of steel and glass. When this was agreed on it gave me an excuse to push for replacing the jaded existing kitchen. The conservatory was added on to the back of the house, covering the full width of the kitchen. As the outside kitchen wall would have to be removed, all the plumbing, electrics and kitchen units would have to be relocated anyway, so the kitchen makeover was not really such an extravagant idea.

The new scheme has transformed a dark, cramped kitchen and small sitting room into a light, spacious living area in which each activity – cooking, eating and relaxing – is integrated with the next. And the expanse of glass in the conservatory means there's no longer a barrier between the garden and the house.

ABOVE LEFT AND RIGHT:
THE OUTSIDE WALL WAS
DEMOLISHED SO THE
NATURAL LIGHT COULD
SWEEP IN FROM THE
GARDEN, ILLUMINATING
EVERY CORNER OF THE NEW
CONSERVATORY AND
KITCHEN.

Planning

For an ambitious project like this you will need an architect to draw up plans. But first discuss your ideas with your local planning authority to see how planning or building regulations may affect what you want to do. This will save time, money and disappointment.

ABOVE RIGHT: THE KITCHEN WINDOW AT THE BACK WAS REMOVED AND THE OPENING KNOCKED THROUGH TO GIVE ACCESS TO THE NEW CONSERVATORY.

RIGHT: DESPITE THE DRAMATIC EFFECT THE CONSERVATORY HAS HAD ON THE INTERIOR, IT DOESN'T TAKE UP MUCH SPACE IN THE GARDEN.

As well as the outside kitchen wall being knocked through, an opening was made in the wall between the living room and kitchen. The other door that led into the kitchen (in the adjacent wall) was then removed and the wall filled in.

As well as the window that had been in the demolished wall, the kitchen had a second window, but this only had a view of the fence and neighbour's house. I replaced that window with glass blocks, which obscure the view and provide privacy but still allow plenty of light into the room.

The cooking area was repositioned next to this area so that the extractor hood could be on an outside wall, and the sink was sited nearby to allow the plumbing to be on this wall. A new dishwasher and the old washing machine were also installed in the same area (see page 69).

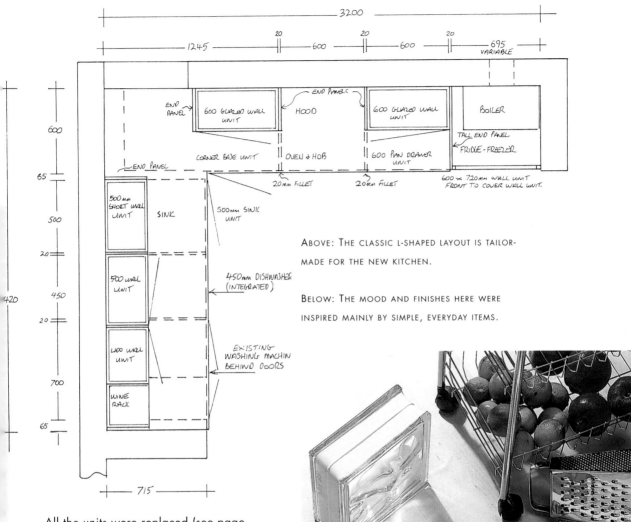

3200

1245 20 600 20 600 20 695 VARIABLE

600

65

500

20

420 450

20

700

65

END PANEL

600 GLAZED WALL UNIT

HOOD

END PANEL

600 GLAZED WALL UNIT

BOILER

TALL END PANEL

FRIDGE-FREEZER

CORNER BASE UNIT

END PANEL

OVEN & HOB

600 PAN DRAWER UNIT

20mm FILLET

20mm FILLET

600 x 720mm WALL UNIT FRONT TO COVER WALL UNIT.

500mm SHORT WALL UNIT

SINK

500mm SINK UNIT

500 WALL UNIT

450mm DISHWASHER (INTEGRATED)

400 WALL UNIT

EXISTING WASHING MACHINE BEHIND DOORS

WINE RACK

715

ABOVE: THE CLASSIC L-SHAPED LAYOUT IS TAILOR-MADE FOR THE NEW KITCHEN.

BELOW: THE MOOD AND FINISHES HERE WERE INSPIRED MAINLY BY SIMPLE, EVERYDAY ITEMS.

All the units were replaced (see page 68). The new, L-shaped layout, consisting of units along the two unbroken walls, is an efficient use of space. There is plenty of storage space in the units, as well as a good length of continuous worktop. The sink, hob, ovens and fridge-freezer are all close to each other, so that the cook doesn't have to walk enormous distances.

Equally important, of course, was the planning of the conservatory itself, as I had to allow for such crucial factors as the direction of the sun and prevailing wind.

The Look

The original kitchen was cluttered and cramped, but had oodles of potential for improvement. Once the walls were removed, the whole ground floor became one massive open space, allowing effortless and unrestricted movement of light. I also

BELOW: THE NEW KITCHEN VIEWED FROM THE CONSERVATORY. THE TURQUOISE AND YELLOW COLOUR SCHEME IS ACCENTED WITH BRIGHTLY COLOURED FLOWERS, FRUITS AND VEGETABLES.

RIGHT: GLASS AND STEEL SURFACES
SHIMMER IN THE NEW KITCHEN,
SEEN HERE FROM THE SITTING ROOM
THROUGH THE NEW OPENING.

BELOW: THE 'BEFORE' SHOT OF THE
PICTURE ON THE RIGHT. THIS IS THE
SITTING ROOM BEFORE THE WALL
BETWEEN IT AND THE KITCHEN WAS
KNOCKED THROUGH TO CONNECT
THE TWO ROOMS.

decided to continue the original sitting room floor into the kitchen and conservatory, reinforcing the feeling of continuous flowing space.

The steel and glass of the conservatory were the keynotes for the look of this kitchen. Steel and other metals predominate, while glass blocks have replaced the window near the hob, and the doors of some of the wall cupboards themselves have sandblasted-glass panels. All this glass allows the natural light to flood in through the conservatory and into the kitchen. Reflecting off the stainless steel and the glazed worktop, it makes the whole living area feel incredibly spacious and airy.

Although the kitchen has the same dimensions as before, it feels much bigger now, not only because of the use of steel and glass but also because of the integrated flooring. Another advantage of the wood was that it helped to prevent the steel and glass looking too clinical.

The basic units are Shaker-style, but the metal handles and the sandblasted glass panels in some of the doors make the units much more individual. So do the brilliant colour of the units and worktop and the large luxuriant plants. The walls of all three areas were painted the same sunny yellow, once again serving to unify the whole scheme.

The Units

With a little thought and planning a practical kitchen doesn't have to be a dull one. It's not hard to adapt a manufacturer's kitchen to your own design and make it unique: just mixing units of differing sizes helps personalize an otherwise standard kitchen.

The kitchen units here were made by a local company and supplied unpainted (see page 70). I decided to break up the line of the wall units so that nothing would be too symmetrical or monotonous. The integral microwave oven, the half-depth shelf over the sink and the built-in wine rack necessitate a varied assortment of door shapes.

A predictable run of wall units was avoided on the adjacent wall, too. Here the extractor hood separates the two main cupboards, while above the refrigerator there is space for a cupboard.

Because the wall units are so varied, the base units could afford to be uniform. They all look identical along the main wall and around the corner as far as the oven. The colour continues for the whole run. One unit was adapted to house the original washing machine behind two doors, and a small dishwasher was installed next to it in another base unit. The doors for these cupboards, along with the door under the sink, all have false drawers for visual unity, to continue the line of the genuine drawers on the adjacent wall.

ABOVE: PUTTING THE MICROWAVE IN A RUN OF WALL UNITS LEAVES THE WORKTOP FREE FOR FOOD PREPARATION. THE MICROWAVE IS ALSO EASIER TO USE WHEN AT EYE LEVEL.

RIGHT: DECIDING TO STOW IT RATHER THAN SHOW IT, WE HOUSED THE ORIGINAL WASHING MACHINE AND NEW DISHWASHER IN BASE UNITS.

The Pyrolave (glazed lavastone) worktop is expensive, but has lots of advantages, including the fact that you can put hot pans on it. You can order it in any colour, so I chose a shade of aqua marginally lighter than the units. It has a Mediterranean feel to it and looks superb.

Paintwork

Buying unpainted kitchen units was a way of keeping costs down. I chose Shaker-style doors but gave them a twist by painting them in a non-traditional colour – a vivid turquoise not available from the manufacturer's standard palette of sober colours – because colour is a potent tool for creating a mood and unifying space.

In order to continue the colour all the way around the working area of the kitchen, I decided to paint the fridge-freezer using the same paint as for the units. Priming metal first with red oxide, an oil-based primer, is essential. (The wooden units have to be primed too, if the manufacturers have not already done so.)

Unclip the unit doors and remove the handles before painting.

> **YOU WILL NEED...**
> Fine-grade sandpaper • Masking tape • Primer (if units not pre-primed) • Oil-based undercoat and top-coat • Small roller and small decorator's brush

PAINTING UNITS

1 Before painting topcoat, lightly sand and then prime all visible wooden surfaces if not pre-primed by manufacturer. (Mask any glass panels with tape.) When dry, apply undercoat. Leave to dry then apply topcoat to recesses of door panels, using brush.

2 Use roller to apply topcoat everywhere else, including sides of drawers. Leave to dry, sand lightly, then apply second coat of top-coat.

ABOVE: THE SANDBLASTED GLASS PANELS OF THE CUPBOARD DOORS FLANKING THE COOKER ADD ANOTHER TEXTURE TO THE UNITS.

RIGHT: RATHER THAN HIDING THE FRIDGE-FREEZER BEHIND CUPBOARD DOORS, WE PAINTED IT TO MATCH.

PAINTING THE FRIDGE

1 Mask parts of fridge you do not want to paint. Protect floor and surrounding area with newspaper; open windows for ventilation. Wearing face mask, spray fridge with primer. Remove tape while primer is damp.

2 When dry, remask portions you will not be painting. Apply topcoat using roller. Remove tape while paint is still damp; allow to dry. Remask and repeat with second coat.

Woodstrip flooring

YOU WILL NEED... *Plastic sheeting (optional) • Cork underlay • Laminated woodstrip 'floating' flooring • Wedges 5–10 mm (1/4–3/8 in) thick • Tenon saw • Moisture-resistant PVA adhesive • Rag • Hammer • Block of wood • Cork expansion strips, or quadrant beading and nails*

The woodstrip flooring used in the conservatory, kitchen and sitting room has a warmth and rich texture that make it a natural counterpoint to the shiny steel and glass surfaces.

A laminated woodstrip 'floating floor' was used. Laid on a cork underlay over the existing floor, it consists of interlocking planks that are glued to each other rather than being fixed to the floor. Laminated wood is easy to clean and is suitable for all three areas, where activities range from cooking and laundry to family meals and entertaining.

HOW TO LAY A 'FLOATING' FLOOR

1 *Make sure floor is dry and level. On concrete, lay plastic sheeting as damp-proof membrane. Cover floor with cork underlay (do not glue or nail it). Shuffle planks before laying, to blend tones.*

2 *Using wedges to leave a 10 mm (⅜ in) expansion gap at each edge, lay row of planks along one wall. Saw last plank to correct length. To glue second row to first, apply adhesive to grooved edge.*

ABOVE: WHERE POSSIBLE, LAY WOODSTRIP FLOORING IN THE DIRECTION OF THE INCOMING LIGHT.

3 *Press planks together, removing excess adhesive with damp rag. If necessary, tap joints tightly closed with hammer (protecting planks with a block of wood).*

4 *Continue until entire floor is covered; last row may have to be cut down in width to fit. Leave for 8 hours. Remove wedges and fit cork expansion strips, or nail quadrant beading to walls (not floor).*

Mobile Storage

Manufacturers these days offer ingenious ways to maximize cupboard space with everything from carousels to deep pot drawers. But few kitchens have all the room for units that their owners need or would like.

This kitchen is no exception: because of the wide openings into the conservatory and sitting room, two sides of this kitchen cannot be used for fitted units. Mobile storage units on castors – in this case a vegetable rack and a trolley made from chromed steel tubing – are ideal in such a situation. Not only do they provide extra shelf space, but they can be moved around to wherever they're needed. The trolley, for instance,

can be wheeled over to the dishwasher to be unloaded, or filled with tableware and food and pushed to the table. With their slightly industrial look, the trolley and vegetable rack are in keeping with the other stainless steel elements in the kitchen, and their contents add attractive splashes of bright colour.

ABOVE: WITH THIS TYPE OF VEGETABLE RACK YOU CAN SEE AT A GLANCE WHAT YOU HAVE ON HAND WHEN YOU START PREPARING A MEAL, AND THE COLOURFUL VEGETABLES ARE ATTRACTIVE IN THEIR OWN RIGHT.

LEFT: THE MOBILE TROLLEY WITH ITS DEEP ADJUST-ABLE SHELVES PROVIDES A GOOD WAY OF STORING ITEMS THAT WOULD NORMALLY TAKE UP VALUABLE PREPARATION SPACE ON THE WORKTOP.

Textures

I designed this kitchen around contrasting 'architectural' textures but I also wanted it to feel like a comfort zone. The highly reflective surfaces of steel, glass and glazed lavastone create an impression of luxury and efficiency, which is softened by the warm tones and wood grain of the flooring and the rich finish of the painted eggshell units.

The stainless steel splashback covers all of the wall between the worktop and wall units. As with the cooker splashback on page 50, it can be custom-made for you if you simply supply a cardboard template. Conventional electrical sockets would have spoiled the effect, so stainless steel was used for them, too – along with

ABOVE: THE SHINY TEXTURES OF THE WORKTOP, THE CHROME TOASTER AND THE GLASS BLOCKS PROVIDE THE PERFECT FOIL FOR FOOD AND PLANTS.

ABOVE: THE GLAZED LAVASTONE WORKTOP WITH ITS PREFORMED SINK MAKES THE WORKING AREA LOOK LIKE ONE GORGEOUS, ENORMOUS GLAZED CERAMIC TILE.

the extractor hood, oven and hob, microwave and handles on the units. Stainless steel or chrome also appears in some of the utensils and accessories. The café-style table and chairs, which can be used both inside and out, are aluminium.

The unusual glazed lavastone worktop reflects back the light from the stainless steel splashback with flashes of warmth. The glass surfaces of the conservatory, the sandblasted-glass door panels and the glass blocks in the old window opening all add subtle textural differences.

RIGHT: THE STAINLESS STEEL SPLASH-
BACK, ENHANCED BY MATCHING
ELECTRICAL SOCKETS AND ACCES-
SORIES LIKE THIS SALAD BOWL, LOOKS
STYLISH AND SOPHISTICATED.

YOU WILL NEED...
*Cardboard at least as large
as splashback • Tape mea-
sure, metre ruler (yardstick)
and felt-tip pen • Scissors •
Masking tape*

HOW TO MAKE A SPLASHBACK TEMPLATE

1 *Carefully measure dimensions of area splashback is
to cover; draw on cardboard.
You will eventually need to
make holes for any electrical
sockets, but at this stage just
notice where they are.*

2 *Check measurements then
cut out, starting with bottom line and holding cardboard up to check it after
cutting each line. Tape in
place. Draw around socket,
then make hole in centre.*

3 *Cut from centre hole out to
each corner. Fold
cardboard triangles back
almost to edge of socket. Cut
off triangles along creases,
leaving hole slightly smaller
than socket.*

UNITS 78

STORAGE 80

WORKTOPS 82

SPLASHBACKS 84

SINKS AND TAPS 86

APPLIANCES 88

LIGHTING 90

FLOORING 92

The *Essentials*

The biggest mistake people make when viewing a kitchen is to see it as a single commodity. If you really think about it, any kitchen is the sum of the different components that make it up. It's a big jigsaw of units, handles, worktops, splashbacks, sinks, taps, appliances, lighting, flooring. Not only the large items are important but also the smaller ones. Details and accessories can make or break a kitchen.

Units

The units are the foundation of your kitchen. When choosing them, you have basically two choices: ready- or custom-made. The construction and composition of most manufacturers' kitchen units are broadly the same. They are generally made from particleboard board, which is compounded wood chips within a laminate surface. Obviously at the top of the range, higher-quality materials and superior craftsmanship are the norm but in the mid price range the composition and construction of the carcasses are broadly similar. Personally, I don't see the logic in purchasing a unit that is built to last a lifetime when you only want it to last for ten years or so, after which it will look dated.

RIGHT: UNMATCHING CUPBOARDS CAN LOOK MORE INTERESTING AND PROVIDE MORE VERSATILE STORAGE. HERE THE CUPBOARDS ARE CONSTRUCTED IN THE SAME WAY AND HAVE SIMILAR CIRCLE MOTIFS, BUT THEIR DIMENSIONS, FINISHES AND HANDLES ARE ALL DIFFERENT.

ABOVE LEFT: THE CONE LEGS ON
THESE UNITS GIVE THE ILLUSION
OF FREESTANDING FURNITURE.

ABOVE: LATTICE WORK ON THE DOORS COMPLEMENTS
THE COUNTRY MOOD OF THIS KITCHEN PERFECTLY.

BELOW: CLASSIC MEETS CONTEMPORARY, WITH
A STRONG INFLUENCE OF BIEDERMEIER
ANTIQUE FURNITURE.

How you dress the units is important, because the doors and handles will determine what your kitchen looks like. Think of the kitchen carcass as a shop dummy – depending on which outfit it wears, it can look countrified, sleek or minimalist.

There are more handles in the kitchen than in any other room in the house, and a good choice of handle can quite literally change a well-designed kitchen into a great one. They not only have to look good but must be pleasing to touch and comfortable to grip as well. If in doubt, buy a selection of different kinds, take them home and Blu-Tack them in place on the unit doors to see which are the most suitable.

Storage

A kitchen is like a woman's handbag. It's never big enough and it's always full of things that are rarely used. You won't be able to work efficiently in the kitchen if items are stored in the wrong place, no matter how well designed the storage space is. Pots and pans hung at head height on the other side of the room from the oven and hob, or cutlery and plates stored far from the sink and dishwasher, will mean chaos in the kitchen. Keep everyday items where you need them.

The food storage in the kitchen should reflect the owners' needs and circumstances. Family

ABOVE: RECYCLING IS A WAY OF LIFE AND NOT A FAD, AND FREESTANDING BINS ARE A SIMPLE SOLUTION.

size, distance from the shops, and whether shopping is done with or without a car, some buying done in bulk, meals prepared in advance and then frozen, fresh or frozen vegetables used, or storage needed for wine are all factors that determine your storage needs.

Poorly positioned shelves in cabinets waste valuable storage space. The shelves in which cans are stored should be closer together than shelves for storing pans. It sounds obvious but very few of us actually adjust the shelving to suit our needs.

LEFT: SHALLOW SHELVES TAKE UP VERY LITTLE SPACE BUT ENSURE THAT COOKING INGREDIENTS ARE IN FULL VIEW AND READILY TO HAND.

BELOW: A FREESTANDING UNIT LIKE THIS RETRO-STYLE VERSION CAN BE TAKEN WITH YOU WHEN YOU MOVE HOUSE.

BELOW: A SLIMLINE PULL-OUT STORAGE UNIT GIVES ALL-ROUND ACCESS TO BOTTLES AND JARS. GOOD VISIBILITY ENSURES THAT THE FOOD CAN BE REGULARLY CHECKED FOR FRESHNESS.

LEFT: THIS STATE-OF-THE-ART ROW OF UNITS CONTAINS EVERY CONCEIVABLE FORM OF STORAGE, INCLUDING APPLIANCE GARAGES AND SHELVES AT VARIABLE DISTANCES APART.

Worktops

In an ideal world every worktop would be attractive, easy to clean, hard-wearing, heat-resistant and able to withstand stains and scratches. But in reality this is far from the case. Different worktop materials have different properties, so choose the one that most suits your needs and budget.

Granite worktops have a natural beauty, are heatproof and waterproof and will withstand most scratches and chips, but they are expensive. The same

ABOVE: LAMINATE IS THE MOST WIDELY USED WORKTOP MATERIAL.

applies to glazed lavastone. Slate is less costly than granité and it too is heatproof and resistant to chips and scratches. However, a sealant has to be applied to make it waterproof, and it's quite susceptible to staining from oil and grease. Another expensive material, terrazzo is a mixture of granite and marble chips set in white cement that has a polished finish.

Ceramic tiles should be avoided as they are prone to crazing and the grout gets dirty and unhygienic.

Hardwood worktops are full of character and are quite reasonably priced, but they are easily marked with knives.

Though expensive, stainless steel gives a professional feel to the kitchen and is

ABOVE LEFT: A CURVED WORKTOP LIKE THIS WOODEN ONE ADDS A SLEEK AND STYLISH DIMENSION TO A KITCHEN.

hygienic, heatproof, waterproof and non-corrosive. The brushed finish is best as it will disguise any scratches.

Laminate, such as Formica, is about to have a revival because of the enormous range of colours, patterns and textures that are available and because it is quite inexpensive. It's also water-resistant and easy to clean, though it can be damaged by cutting. The most common type comes with a post-formed (rounded) edge.

A solid-surface material, such as Corian, which is made from synthetic resin, is smooth and seamless and so is ideal around the sink area, especially if the sink itself is made from it too (see page 87). It is water- and heat-resistant, hygienic – and expensive.

ABOVE: GLAZED LAVASTONE SUCH AS PYROLAVE CAN BE MADE IN ANY COLOUR. THOUGH EXPENSIVE, IT LOOKS SENSATIONAL.

ABOVE: IF YOU HAVE ANY LEFTOVER WORKTOP, GET SOME LEGS AND MAKE YOURSELF A COORDINATING TABLE.

RIGHT: DIFFERENT WORKTOP MATERIALS CAN BE USED WHERE THEY ARE MOST SUITABLE. HERE GRANITE INSERTS ARE IDEAL FOR CHOPPING BOARDS.

Splashbacks

Splashbacks are well-named as they have to take a serious amount of splashing and are used to protect the wall surfaces that take the most abuse from cooking and cleaning. Ordinary wallpaper or paint would soon succumb to the steam and splashes that food preparation and cooking generate. Splashbacks should be easy to clean, heat-resistant and waterproof and should look gorgeous.

Because the area of a splashback is small in proportion to the rest of the kitchen, using an extravagant material for it is actually very cost-effective, since you can have a really great splashback material for an amount that won't necessitate a visit to the bank manager.

ABOVE: THIS PAINTED SPLASHBACK GIVES YOU ORIGINALITY AND SAVES YOU A FORTUNE.

BELOW: SLEEK STAINLESS STEEL GIVES A COOL AIR OF URBAN CHIC.

The most popular splashback material is manufactured tiles. Their advantages are that they are economical, easy to clean and heat-resistant, but their disadvantage is that the regular shape of the tiles can become hellishly monotonous. Handmade tiles, although much more expensive than manufactured ones, look a hundred times sexier with their irregular sizes and vivid colours.

Mosaic (see page 20) is a conventional alternative to the larger tiles. Treated slates (see page 36) give a textured feel to splashbacks. Granite can also be used, as can stainless steel (see page 74).

The least expensive splashback alternative is to paint a design of your choice,

either freehand or perhaps using a
stencil, on the wall in matt emulsion
paint, and then protect it with several
coats of acrylic varnish.

Another alternative is to use laminated
worktop. This can be quite effective
placed upright directly against the walls,
with the rounded edge at the top.

RIGHT: THE UNEVENNESS AND WONDERFUL
COLOURS OF HAND-MADE TILES LITERALLY GIVE
THEM THE EDGE OVER MANUFACTURED TILES.

Sinks and Taps

Who likes washing up? I certainly don't, but the washing up area is used more than anywhere else in the kitchen, whether for washing up itself or for food preparation, unless you've got your own kitchen fairy.

It's very important for the sink to be at the right height and the washing bowl to be of the correct depth; otherwise, working in this area is awkward and uncomfortable.

Before deciding on what sink unit to have, consider what tasks it will be used for. A double sink allows dirty dishes to be soaked in one bowl while fresh produce is rinsed in the other. A compact single-bowl sink without a drainer is ideal for minimal usage and ease of rinsing prior to loading the dishwasher. Units with double drainers and units with half-bowls are also available, and most sink units come in either left- or right-handed versions.

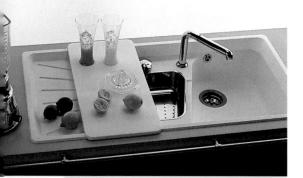

ABOVE: ALL SORTS OF ACCESSORIES ARE AVAILABLE TO FIT INTO SINK UNITS, INCLUDING CHOPPING BOARDS, DRAINING RACKS AND COLANDER BASKETS.

ABOVE: AN ELEGANT TWO-BOWL CORNER SINK, WITH A CENTRAL TAP, IS ONE OF THE CLEVEREST DESIGNS AROUND.

RIGHT: STAINLESS STEEL UNDERHUNG SINKS ARE IDEAL FOR SETTING INTO GRANITE WORKTOPS. HARD-WEARING AND HYGIENIC, STAINLESS STEEL IS STILL ONE OF THE MOST PRACTICAL AND POPULAR MATERIALS FOR A SINK. A ONE-AND-A-HALF-BOWL SINK UNIT LIKE THIS PROVIDES THE FLEXIBILITY OF A FULL DOUBLE SINK BUT TAKES UP LESS SPACE.

If you don't have a dishwasher, then the washing bowl and draining board should ideally be made of a material that will lessen the chances of breakages, such as stainless steel or composite.

The monobloc mixer tap with its single spout and single taphole is the most popular choice for the modern kitchen, as the water temperature is controlled through the one outlet. For a traditional style feature, investigate replica old-style pillar taps or buy originals from a salvage yard.

There is an old-wives' tale put about by many designers, mostly male, who insist that the sink be located in front of a window so that the little woman can have a nice view as she whiles away the hours at the sink. On the rare occasions when I'm at the sink, I watch what I'm doing and finish the chore as quickly as possible. Position the sink wherever you want to.

ABOVE: THE BELFAST SINK, MADE OF PORCELAIN-COATED FIRECLAY, IS AN OLD-FASHIONED DESIGN THAT IS WIDE AND DEEP.

ABOVE: CORIAN SINKS, DRAINERS AND WORKTOPS ARE JOINED WITH INVISIBLE SEAMS, MAKING THEM ESPECIALLY HYGIENIC.

Appliances

The look and quality of appliances can be the icing on the cake for your kitchen. There is a terrible snobbery surrounding which make of appliance you use. In my experience, comparing efficiency, reliability, looks and cost can throw up all sorts of surprises. Often the big names don't live up to expectations. Consider how you will use the appliance and what you expect it to do for you. Decide whether you want your appliances to be on view or integrated by having similar doors to those on the units.

Ovens come in all shapes and sizes, so think about how much you are likely

BELOW: GLASS-DOOR REFRIGERATION IS ULTRA-GLAMOROUS BUT ALSO INCREDIBLY PRACTICAL, EVEN IF IT MEANS KEEPING THE INSIDE IMMACULATELY TIDY.

ABOVE: CURVES ARE THE SHAPE OF THINGS TO COME. AT LAST, FLUID AND SENSUOUS LINES ARE BEGINNING TO APPEAR IN APPLIANCES.

to use it, whether it needs a large capacity and whether you want it to be self-cleaning. Consider the position carefully, too. A low-level oven can be more awkward for looking inside and taking dishes out of than an eye-level one, but is the best for saving space. Hobs must be easy to clean and should have pan grids that are stable.

Problems with condensation and cooking smells will all but disappear if you choose the correct extractor. The shop will tell you the cubic capacity you need, based on the length, width and height of your kitchen. Check that the fan runs fairly quietly and that there is a task light under the hood.

When deciding on a fridge or freezer, consider whether you just keep a bag of frozen peas and ice cream, or freeze home produce.

BELOW: A RETRO REVIVAL: OLD-STYLE APPLIANCE SHAPES ARE MAKING A COMEBACK, BUT IN BRIGHT COLOURS THIS TIME ROUND.

ABOVE: THE BLAND AND BORING OVEN GETS A NEW STREAMLINED SIMPLICITY. A DESIGN FIT FOR SPACE EXPLORATION.

RIGHT: SOME COOKS LIKE TO HAVE TWO DIFFERENT TYPES OF HEAT SOURCE. WHAT BETTER COMBINATION THAN THE FOUR CERAMIC RINGS AND TWO GAS ONES IN THIS CLEVER HOB?

Lighting

Lights! Action! Without decent lighting you'll never cook up a storm in the kitchen. It may seem obvious but you're not going to make the finest delicacies if you can't see what you are up to. A balance has to be struck between style and function.

The kitchen requires both task and ambient lighting. Task lighting, as the name implies, is needed for work areas. It improves visibility and helps you to concentrate on what you're doing. Ambient lighting is in the background and is used for general lighting in the kitchen. Try flooding a corner of your kitchen with light for an instant summer feel all the year round.

Task lights should be located over the hob, sink and work surface. Low-voltage halogen lights are ideal. Extractor hoods usually have lights fitted underneath the

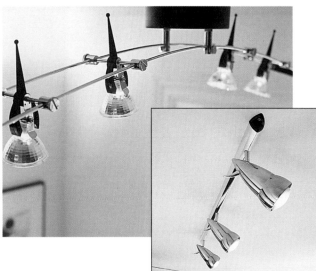

LEFT AND INSET: THE POSITIONS OF THESE TRACK SPOTLIGHTS CAN BE ADJUSTED WITHOUT HAVING TO DO ANY REWIRING, USING AN ALREADY EXISTING FIXED CEILING POINT. TRACK LIGHTING COMES IN VARIOUS STYLES – CHOOSE ONE TO SUIT YOUR KITCHEN.

ABOVE: SIMPLE, INEXPENSIVE LIGHT BULBS, PLACED SYMMETRICALLY, CAN LOOK IMPRESSIVE.

LEFT: HALF A DOZEN HALOGEN DOWNLIGHTERS RECESSED INTO THE CEILING PROVIDE GOOD WORKTOP LIGHTING IN THIS KITCHEN.

canopy to light the hob, while lights fitted underneath the wall-mounted units will illuminate the worktop and sink area.

Ambient lighting can be provided by a ceiling light or wall lights that wash over the whole kitchen.

The reflective properties of many of the appliances and utensils found in the kitchen can provide a dramatic backdrop to the room's lighting. Stainless steel, chrome and ceramic tiles all have reflective qualities and offer a major opportunity to influence the atmosphere.

LEFT: RECESSED HALOGEN DOWN-LIGHTERS AND TRACKLIGHTS ILLU-MINATE THIS LONG, NARROW KITCHEN, SUPPLE-MENTED BY A LIGHT IN THE EXTRACTOR ABOVE THE HOB.

Flooring

Flooring is often the last thing you think of when revamping the kitchen but its importance shouldn't be underestimated. The common mistake is to go for a neutral, inoffensive, boring floor. Why have that when you can have floor fantastic?

Confidence is needed when looking at all the alternatives. Bear in mind that it will need to be hard-wearing, hygienic, affordable and good-looking. If the floor area is large enough, you might consider two flooring finishes, to add interest – perhaps a very durable finish like ceramic tiles near the sink and oven and a softer vinyl on the rest. Large tiles work well on a large floor, as small tiles look too fussy.

ABOVE: WOOD LAMINATE FLOORING GIVES A PLEASING MODERN SIMPLICITY. LONG-LASTING AND WARM UNDERFOOT, IT IS RELATIVELY EASY TO INSTALL (SEE PAGE 72).

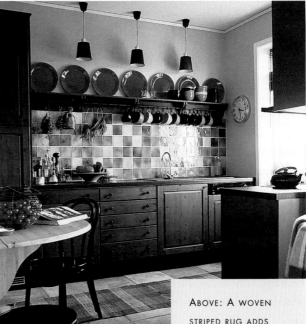

ABOVE: A WOVEN STRIPED RUG ADDS WARMTH TO THE FEEL-GOOD STONE FLOOR.

LEFT: VIVID COLOURS AND
DESIGNS ARE AVAILABLE IN
RUBBER, LAMINATES AND PVC-
COATED CORK TILES.

RIGHT: MARBLE FLOORING IS
OFTEN REGARDED AS THE
ULTIMATE CHOICE. IT REFLECTS
LIGHT BUT CAN BE VERY COLD
UNDERFOOT.

I recommend that you lay your flooring after the units are installed. Leave the plinths off the units so that the flooring will go underneath them by a small distance. In this way not only do you save a fortune on the material that would otherwise be wasted under the units, but your floor will also be in pristine condition because it won't have had workmen building the kitchen on top of it.

Ceramic tiles and slate are hard-wearing but can be cold underfoot unless you have underfloor heating. Wooden floors are warm but require maintenance, particularly around the sink, where water damage may occur. Modern materials like vinyl, linoleum and laminates are very adaptable and usually have all the qualities necessary for a kitchen floor. Linoleum can be fitted to your own design but it must be installed by an expert.

ABOVE: TWO NATURAL PRODUCTS, LIMESTONE AND
WOOD, ARE USED TO PRODUCE A COMBINATION
KITCHEN FLOOR.

Acknowledgements

THE SMALL KITCHEN (PAGES 12–25)

Kitchen units Metod style, *worktop, sink, tap, wooden display boxes:* IKEA, tel: 0181 208 5600 for nearest store.

Cooker Cannon Pearl Duo: Creda Ltd, PO Box 5, Creda Works, Blythe Bridge, Stoke on Trent ST11 9LJ, tel: 01782 388 388.

Dishwasher Model DH101: Tricity Bendix, tel: 0990 805 805 for stockists.

Extractor Philips Whirlpool; available nationwide, tel: 0181 649 500.

Handles Dimple 2602: MGA Interserve Ltd, Unit 17, Sapcote Trading Estate, Powke Lane, Cradley Heath, West Midlands B64 5QR, tel: 01384 638 700.

Mosaic tiles Mosaic Workshop, Unit B, 443–449 Holloway Road, London N7 6LJ, tel: 0171 263 2997.

Cork floor tiles B&Q, tel: 01703 256 256 for nearest stores.

Roller blinds by Alison White; Novatec, Star Lane, Margate, Kent CT9 4EF, tel: 01843 604 430.

Shelving unit Aero, 96 Westbourne Grove, London, W2 5RT, tel: 0171 221 1950.

Accessories, sweeping brush, shopping bag Emma Bernhardt, 301 Portobello Road, London, W10, tel: 0181 960 2929.

Toaster Ocean, tel: 0800 132 985 order line.

Storage jars, popcorn boxes, griddle Lakeland Ltd, Alexandra Buildings, Windermere, Cumbria, LA23 1BQ, tel: 01539 488 100 mail order.

Kitchen fitter Martin Butler, tel: 0589 479 373.

Tiler Scott Philips, tel: 0976 805 669.

PAINTS & VARNISHES
Cabinet stripes 67RB21/342, 45RB44/242 and white all in satinwood finish: Dulux, tel: 01753 550 000 for stockists.

Floor White and 39RB34124 matt emulsion: Dulux, as above
Floor Acrylic eggshell varnish: Craig & Rose, 172 Leith Walk, Edinburgh EH6 5EB, tel: 0131 554 1131.

THE FAMILY KITCHEN (PAGES 26–43)

Kitchen units Woburn range; kitchen appliances; computerized plans: Wickes, tel: 0500 300 328 for nearest store.

Reclaimed slates and floorboards Lassco, 101–108 Britannia Walk, London N1 7LU, tel: 0171 252 5157.

Belfast sink Twyfords Caradon Bathrooms, Lawton Road, Alsager, Stoke on Trent, Staffs ST7 2DF, tel: 01270 879 777.

Tap Nu Line Ltd, 315 Westbourne Park Road, London W11 1EF, tel: 0171 727 7748.

Self adhesive floor tiles Spectrum Harmony: Homebase, tel: 0181 784 7200 for nearest store.

Handles on units; *hinges* on shutters, Rough at the Edge range: Clayton Munroe, Kingston, Staverton, Totnes, Devon, TQ9 6AR, tel: 01803 762 626.

Fretwork shutters on windows, Schedar design number 45: Jali Ltd, Apsley House, Chartham, Canterbury, Kent, CT4 7HT, tel: 01227 831 710.

Grey primer spray paint on shutters Plasti Kote Ltd, tel: 01223 836 400.

Chairs Designers Guild, 267–271 King's Road, London, SW3 5EN, tel: 0171 351 5775.

Ceiling light Pronto Arch; *pan rack:* John Lewis plc, tel: 0171 629 7711 for nearest store.

Baskets Holding Company, Unit 15, Imperial Studio, 3–11 Imperial Road, London SW6 2AG, tel: 0171 610 9166.

Kettle, fan, pancake griddle Divertimenti, 139–141 Fulham Road, London SW3 6SD, tel: 0171 581 8065.

Crockery The Pier, tel: 0171 814 5004 order line.

Computer drawings Martin Meredith at Wickes, 120-138 Station Rd, Harrow, Middx MA1 2QB, tel: 0181 901 200.

Kitchen fitter and decorator Martin Butler as above.

Electrics Keith Fuller, tel: 0181 330 0620 and 0802 346 282.

Plumbing Greg Demosthenous, tel: 0973 152 362.

PAINTS & VARNISHES
Cabinets Red Rooster & Yellow 20YY46 1515 matt emulsion: Dulux as above; *walls* Braided Straw matt emulsion: Dulux as above; *skirtings* Black satinwood: Dulux as above; *Table glaze* Rustins Blue Colourglaze: Leyland Paints Ltd, tel: 0800 454 484 for nearest stockists; *Cabinets* Acrylic eggshell varnish: Craig & Rose as above.

THE COOK'S KITCHEN (PAGES 44–61)

Kitchen units Eton Maple and green effect, worktop, white enamel sink, integrated fridge-freezer, parquet flooring: Wickes, tel: 0500 300 328 for nearest store.

Cooker SUK854X: Smeg UK, Corinthian Court, 80 Milton Park, Abingdon, Oxon, OX14; available from Hot & Cold, tel: 0181 960 1300.

Extractor MFI, tel: 0800 192 192 for nearest store.

Stainless steel splashback Paramount Industries, 246 Kilburn Lane, London W10 4DA, tel: 0181 960 0666.

Granite worksurface Marble & Granite Trading Company, Unit 4, Bush Industrial Estate,15–25 Standard Road, London NW10 6DF, tel: 0181 453 1166.

Hanging rack for saucepans Richard Needham, 23 Lodge Avenue, Dartford, Kent DA1 3DX, tel: 01322 224 228.

Tiles on splashback Fired Earth, Twyford Mill, Oxford Road, Adderbury, Oxon OX17 3HP, tel: 01295 812 088 for nearest supplier.

Pull-out bin mechanism, castors on mobile unit: Nu Line as above.

Halogen wire track light, utensils, lazy susan, hanging cookbook and spice rack, tea cloths IKEA, tel: 0181 208 5600 for nearest store

Utensil hanging grid, wine rack, bread board and accessories Lakeland Ltd as above.

Saucepans Divertimenti as above.

PAINTS & VARNISHES
Walls Gardenia matt emulsion; window Park Side satinwood; parquet floor diluted Park Side matt emulsion: all from Dulux as above.

Parquet floor Acrylic eggshell varnish: Craig & Rose as above.

THE GLASS KITCHEN (PAGES 62–75)

Conservatory City Aluminium Ltd, Unit 2, Acorn Industrial Estate, Crayford Road, Dartford, Kent DA1 4AL, tel: 01322 522 357.

Kitchen units Plymouth Shaker style; handles: Winchmore Premium Kitchens, Unit 5, Business Park, Northgate Street, Bury St Edmunds, Suffolk 1P33 1HP, tel: 01284 724 207.

Worktop and sink in glazed lavastone Pyrolave, Hollybush Lane, Bendish, Herts SG4 8JB Tel: 01438 871 047.

Tap monobloc single lever: Bergen, Tel: 0181 205 1133 for suppliers.

Oven ZBS703SS; hob ZBG502SS; extractor CWH6O6SS: Zanussi, tel: 0990 140 140 or www.zanussi.con.

Microwave H5453 integrated; dishwasher 450ML integrated: Neff Appliances, tel: 01908 328 300 for stockists.

Stainless steel splashbacks Denton Commercial Kitchen Supplies, tel: 0171 622 7157 for stockists.

Flooring Wicanders, Amorim House, Star Road, Partridge Green, Horsham, West Sussex, tel: 01403 710 001.

Glass blocks Wickes as above.

Sandblasted glass in units: Abbots Glass, 101–103a Victoria Road,

Ruislip Manor, Middlesex HA4 9BN, tel: 01895 633 333.

Chrome trolley, chrome vegetable rack and accessories Lakeland Ltd as above.

Table, chairs, plants, crockery IKEA, tel: 0181 208 5600 for nearest store.

Lighting Kontinental Housecraft Ltd, Bearwalden House, Wendens Ambo, Saffron Walden, Essex CB11 4JX, tel: 0179 954 1175.

Building work Milestone Construction; Dave Price, tel: 0976 426 039.

Interior paintwork Mark Biggins, tel: 0181 577 5532.

Electrics Keith Fuller, tel: 0181 330 0620 & 0802 346 282

PAINTS
Walls Nugget Gold JK250 matt emulsion and Twenty Carats K360 matt emulsion: Crown, tel: 01254 704 951 for stockists; Units Savanna eggshell: Sanderson, tel: 01895 238 244 for stockists.

Thanks to Nicky Copeland, Gabrielle, Rona and Lucy at Phoebus Editions, Anthea Morton-Saner, Daisy Goodwin, Simon Shaw, Inga Schulze, Kay Hawkins, Martin Butler, John Duckworth, Greg Demosthenous, Keith Fuller, Scott Phillips, Martin Meredith at Wickes, Michael Kamlish, William Martin at Ikea, Richard Fullbrook at Winchmore, Camron PR for Homebase, Michelle Kershaw at Lakeland Ltd, Jo Thiel for Dulux, Colin Mitchell-Rose at Craig & Rose, Sarah McAvoy for MFI and everyone in the Home Front office. Thanks also to the kitchen owners – Geraldine Monaghan, Diane and Stuart Blandamer, Paula and Noel O'Reilly, and Brian and Emma Wares – and to all the suppliers who kindly helped out with the projects.

PICTURE CREDITS

BBC Books would like to thank the following for providing photographs and for permission to reproduce copyright material. While every effort has been made to trace and acknowledge all copyright holders, we would like to apologize should there have been any errors or omissions.
Page 1 Robert Harding Picture Library (S. Gillien/Ideal Home); Page 7 Robert Harding Picture Library (Tom Leighton/Options); Page 8 (t) Anne McKevitt, (cl) Magnet Ltd; Page 9 (t) Robert Harding Picture Library (Simon Brown/Country Homes & Interiors), (b) Robert Harding Picture Library (Geoffrey Frosh/Homes & Gardens); Page 61 (tr & br) IKEA; Page 77 (tl) Martin Moore & Company, (tr) Bosch Kitchens, (bl) Alno, (br) Elizabeth Whiting & Assocs (Rodney Hyett); Page 78 (b) Robert Harding Picture Library (Trevor Richards/Homes & Gardens); Page 78-9 (t) Bosch Kitchens; Page 79 (t) Robert Harding Picture Library (S. Gillien/Ideal Home), (b) Robinson & Cornish; Page 80 (t) Lakeland Ltd, (c & b) SieMatic; Page 81 (tr) Robert Harding Picture Library (Tony Timmington/Ideal Home), (bl) Alno, (br) Chromagene Ltd; Page 82 (tr) Alno, (bl) Bosch Kitchens; Page 83 (t) Pyrolave, (cl) Magnet Ltd, (br) Elizabeth Whiting & Assocs (Rodney Hyett); Page 84 (t) Anne McKevitt (Colin Poole), (b) Capricorn Kitchens; Page 85 (t) Elizabeth Whiting & Assocs (Rodney Hyett), (b) Anne McKevitt (Colin Poole); Page 86 Blanco; Page 87 (tr) Martin Moore & Company, (bl) Blanco, (br) Dupont Corian; Page 88 (t) Zanussi, (b) Simon Kenny/Belle/Arcaid; Page 89 (bl) Bosch Domestic Appliances, (tr) Miele, (br) Alno; Page 90 (bl and inset) IKEA; Page 90-1 Elizabeth Whiting & Assocs (Rodney Hyett); Page 91 (t) Elizabeth Whiting & Assocs (Michael Dunne), (b) Robert Harding Picture Library (Bill Reavell/Homes & Ideas); Page 92,(bl) Pergo, (br) IKEA; Page 93 (t) SieMatic, (b) Robert Harding Picture Library (Jonathan Pilkington/Homes & Gardens). All other photographs © BBC Books.

Index

A appliances, 88–9

B Belfast sinks, 30, 38, 87
bins:
    recycling, 61, 80
    waste, pull-out, 57
blinds, 17

C colourwashing:
    parquet flooring, 58
    pine units, 32–4
conservatory kitchen, 62–75
cookers, 48–50, 88, 89
Cook's Kitchen, 44–61
Corian, 83, 87
cork floor tiles, painted, 24–5
country-style kitchen, modern,
    26–43
cupboards, *see* larders *and* units

D dishwashers, 55
display boxes, 22–3

E electrical sockets, 56, 57, 74, 75
extractors, 50, 89

F family kitchen, 26–43
flooring, 92–3
    colourwashed parquet, 58
    laminated woodstrip, 72
    painted cork, 24–5
    preparing sub-floor, 42
    vinyl, 42–3

G glass, sandblasted, 67, 70
glass blocks, 64, 74
Glass Kitchen, 62–75
granite:
    splashbacks, 84
    worktops and inserts, 53, 82, 83

H handles, 19, 35, 79
hobs, 88, 89

L laminate:
    splashbacks, 85
    units, 52–3
    wood flooring, 72, 92

worktops, 82, 83
larders:
    pull-out, 53, 81
    understairs cupboard 59
lavastone, glazed, 68, 74, 82, 83
lighting, 56–7, 90–1
linoleum, 93

M mobile units, 52–3, 61
mosaic splashbacks, 20–1, 84

O ovens, 88, 89

P painting:
    cork floor tiles, 24–5
    pine units, 32–4
    Shaker-style units, 70
    splashbacks, 84, 85
    stripes on units, 18–19
    see also colourwashing *and* table,
        staining
particleboard, 78
peninsula unit, 28, 29
pictures, leaf, 39
planning, 8–9
    cook's kitchen, 46–7
    family kitchen, 28-9
    glass kitchen, 64–5
    small kitchen, 14–15
Pyrolave, *see* lavastone, glazed

R racks:
    saucepan, 39
    spice, 49
    utensil, 55
    vegetable, 73
    vinegar, 54
    wine, 68
recycling bins, 80
refrigerators, 88, 89
    painting, 70, 71

S shutters, 40
sinks, 30, 38, 55, 74, 86–7
slate, 31, 37, 82, 84, 92
Small Kitchen, 12–25
splashbacks, 84–5
    mosaic, 20–1, 84
    slate, 31, 37, 84

stainless steel, 50, 74, 75, 84
tiled, 51, 84, 85
stainless steel:
    sinks, 86
    splashbacks, 50, 74, 75, 84
    worktops, 82
storage, 22–3, 49, 80–1
    hanging, 39, 49, 55
    mobile, 52–3, 61, 73
    see also units
stripes, painting, 18–19

T table, staining, 41
taps, 38, 55, 84–5
template, splashback, 74, 75
tiles, ceramic:
    floor, 92
    splashbacks, 51, 84, 85
    worktops, 82
    see also mosaic splashbacks
trolley, 73

U units, 78–9
    mobile, 52–3, 61
    painted and colourwashed pine,
        32–4
    painted Shaker-style, 70
    peninsula, 28, 29
    pull-out, 53, 57, 81
    striped, 18–19
    woodgrain laminate, 52–3
utility room annexe, 44, 60–1

V vinyl flooring, 42–3, 92

W windows, 40
    bare, 54
    blinds, 17
    glass blocks, 64, 74
    shutters, 40
wood:
    floors, 58, 72, 93
    worktops, 30–1, 36–7, 82
worktops, 82-3
    extra-deep, 54
    fold-down, 17
    glazed lavastone, 68, 74, 82, 83
    granite, 53, 82, 83
    wood, 30–1, 36–7, 82